AMERICAN CITIES CHRONOLOGY SERIES

NEWARK
A CHRONOLOGICAL & DOCUMENTARY HISTORY

1666-1970

Compiled and Edited by
ARNOLD S. RICE

Series Editor
HOWARD B. FURER

1977
OCEANA PUBLICATIONS, INC.
Dobbs Ferry, New York

For my son Noah Bruce

Library of Congress Cataloging in Publication Data

Rice, Arnold S.
  Newark: a chronological & documentary history,
1666-1970.

  (American cities chronology series)
  Bibliography: p.
  Includes index.
  SUMMARY: A chronology of important events in the
history of Newark accompanied by pertinent documents.
  1. Newark, N.J. — History — Chronology.
2. Newark, N.J. — History — Sources. [1. Newark,
N.J. — History]
F144.N657R53   974.9'32   77-23412
ISBN 0-379-00608-1

MAY 1 1978

TABLE OF CONTENTS

EDITOR'S FOREWORD

The purpose of this undertaking is to provide within a single volume the following material on Newark, New Jersey: a. the pertinent facts about the city, arranged chronologically; b. representative documents conveying the political, economic and social flavor of the city at various periods; c. a comprehensive bibliography of both the primary sources and secondary works relating to the city.

The greatest care has been exercized to list accurately the year, month, and day for each entry in the Chronology. For some events in the early period of Newark's existence the precise dates have not been successfully traced because documentation is either lacking or conflicting. Where this is the case, only the year or the year and month are given.

Arnold S. Rice
Kean College of New Jersey

THE SEVENTEENTH CENTURY

1666   May. Newark was settled (according to tra-
        dition on the eighteenth day of this month)
        by thirty Puritan families led by Robert
        Treat. The settlers had left New Haven Col-
        ony because of discontent with its incorpora-
        tion into Connecticut Colony two years ear-
        lier.

1667   June 24. The residents decided to elect an-
        nually from among themselves the officials
        who would govern the community.

1668   May 20. Representatives from Newark and E-
        lizabeth (then called Elizabethtown) convened
        to define the boundaries between the adjoining
        communities.

        September 10. The residents decided to build
        their first church, known as the "Meeting
        House," which was soon erected on Broad
        Street.

1669   January. A judicial system was established,
        consisting of two court sessions held annual-
        ly, with verdicts being rendered by a jury
        composed of six male residents. This plan
        was to be in effect for three years.

        June 17. The judicial system was revised to
        embody the holding of four sessions annually.

1673   September 6. All male residents between the
        ages of sixteen and sixty were ordered to
        assemble with their weapons because of dan-
        ger to the community from the hostile behav-
        ior of nearby Indians.

        September 14. With the English surrender of
        New York to the Netherlands, the control of
        New Jersey by the Dutch had begun. Upon the
        demand of a transfer of allegiance by New
        Jersey inhabitants from England to the Ne-
        therlands, seventy-five of the eighty-six
        male residents (eleven were absent at the
        time) of Newark took the prescribed oath to
        the new government. The following February,
        New Jersey was restored by the Netherlands
        to England.

1675   August 28. In anticipation of trouble with
        the Indians, the residents decided to outfit

the church to serve as a place of defense
for the community.

1676   February 6. The authorities forbade under
a penalty of ten shillings the cutting down
of trees that were designated for purposes
of shade (thus in effect establishing Newark's first shade tree commission).

1679   March 29. After Sir Edmund Andros, governor
of New York, had assumed authority over New
Jersey on behalf of the Duke of York, the
brother of King Charles II of England, the
residents of Newark, resenting Andros' inter-
ference, replied to him that they had taken
an oath of allegiance to the king, and until
they had contrary instructions from the mon-
arch, they would remain faithful to the existing form of government.

1682   The population was approximately five hundred.

1691   February 20. Welfare aid was extended for
the first time to a poor resident.

1695   The first saw mill was erected.

1698   The first tanning business was established
by Azariah Crane.

THE EIGHTEENTH CENTURY

1713   April 27. Newark was granted a charter by
Queen Anne of Great Britain.

1714   The first school house was in operation.

1719   November 20. A system of assessing residents
for the support of the poor was established.

1721   Stone was being quarried in the area for the
construction of buildings.

1746   January 13. Repeating an action taken the
preceding year, a mob broke into the jail
and released persons held because of land
suits in favor of the British proprietors.

February 10. Trinity Episcopal Church was
granted a charter by King George II of Great
Britain.

1748   November 9. The first commencement of the
            College of New Jersey (subsequently renamed
            Princeton University) took place in Newark.
            Founded in Elizabeth two years earlier to
            train ministers in evangelical Presbyter-
            ianism, the institution had moved in 1748
            to Newark, where it remained for eight years
            before being established in what is now
            Princeton, New Jersey.

1756   February 6. Aaron Burr, who was to become
            vice president of the United States, was
            born in Newark, where his father served as
            president of the College of New Jersey.

1761   May 13. The first lodge of Free Masons in
            New Jersey was organized in Newark, with its
            initial quarters in the Rising Sun Tavern.

1767   September 9. Formalized horse racing began
            in New Jersey with a contest held at Newark.

1774   December 7. The residents established the
            Committee of Observation to deal with in-
            creasing tensions between the American col-
            onies and Great Britain.

1775   January 4. The Newark Academy, founded in
            the preceding year, opened with formal ex-
            ercises.

            April 24. After having received news of
            the battles of Lexington and Concord, the
            members of the Committee of Observation a-
            dopted a resolution that they were "willing
            at this alarming crisis to risk their lives
            and fortunes in support of American liberty."

            May 8. The townspeople enthusiastically
            greeted various members, including John
            Adams and John Hancock, of the Massachusetts,
            Connecticut, and New York delegations to
            the Second Continental Congress as they made
            their way to Philadelphia, Pennsylvania, for
            the opening session of that body.

            June 25. George Washington passed through
            on his way from Philadelphia, Pennsylvania,
            where he had been a delegate to the Second
            Continental Congress, to assume command of
            the Continental Army at Cambridge, Massa-
            chusetts.

1776   November 28. George Washington and approx-
             imately three thousand troops withdrew from
             Newark, where they had been stationed for
             six days, just hours before Lord Cornwallis
             and about six thousand British troops marched
             into town.

1777   The number of dwellings was 141.

1780   The population was approximately one thou-
             sand.

             January 25. British troops attacked the
             town, burning the Newark Academy, where A-
             merican troops had been quartered, and tak-
             ing prisoner a number of leading residents.

1787   January 4. The first recorded burglary took
             place. Individuals broke into the post of-
             fice at Broad and Market streets and stole
             the mail.

1788   July 4. The first recorded Independence
             Day celebration, which included a parade
             honoring the trades of the town, such as
             weaving, silversmithing, tanning, and clock-
             making, took place.

1791   January 1. The First Presbyterian Church was
             dedicated.

             May 6. The first recorded court-ordered
             execution, in which William Jones was hanged
             for murder, took place.

             May 13. The first issue of Wood's Newark
             Gazette, the earliest newspaper of Newark,
             appeared.

1794   The first free vocational school (probably
             the earliest in the United States) began
             operations, having been sponsored by Moses
             N. Combs, the founder of Newark's shoe in-
             dustry.

             March 19. It appears that at a meeting in
             Seabury's Tavern the Democratic party in
             Newark took shape.

             April 14. Springfield Township was formed
             in part from a portion of Newark.

1796   October 5. The first issue of the Sentinel

of Freedom appeared.

1797   January 26. The first corps of fire-fighters, named the Fire Association, was established.

July 4. The first musical band composed of townspeople participated in the annual Independence Day celebration.

August 2. President John Adams paid a visit to Newark on his way from the nation's capital, Philadelphia, Pennsylvania, to his home in Quincy, Massachusetts.

1798   February 16. Caldwell Township was formed almost entirely from a portion of Newark.

July 10. The Voluntary Association of the People of Newark to Observe the Sabbath was established.

THE NINETEENTH CENTURY

1804   There were 844 houses, 207 craftsmen's shops, and five public buildings; among the residents were ten physicians, fourteen lawyers, nine clergymen, sixteen teachers, thirty-four merchants, and eighty-one farmers.

May 4. The first bank, The Newark Banking and Insurance Company (subsequently renamed The National Newark and Essex Bank), was formed at a meeting in Gifford's Tavern attended by a group of businessmen possessing a charter granted by the New Jersey legislature three months earlier.

1806   Shoe manufacturing was already the leading industry, with approximately one-third of the townspeople employed in it.

November 27. Orange Township (which initially included most of the present Orange, West Orange, East Orange, South Orange, Maplewood, and approximately half of Irvington) was formed entirely from a portion of Newark.

1810   According to the census report of the United States government, the population was 8,008.

The first hat manufacturing business was established by William Rankin.

January 30. A call was issued to people desirous of insuring their property to meet for action, leading to the founding of the Newark Fire Insurance Company the following year.

1812   During the War of 1812 one out of seven men was drafted into military service. Also, a company of approximately nine hundred volunteer riflemen was organized under the command of attorney Theodore Frelinghuysen.

January 24. Bloomfield Township (which initially included the present Montclair, Bloomfield, Glen Ridge, Nutley, and Belleville) was formed entirely from a portion of Newark.

June 2. The State Bank of Newark (subsequently renamed The First National State Bank of New Jersey) opened for business.

1815   The farm of Aaron Johnson was purchased by the town to be used for the care of the poor.

1819   The first patent leather in the nation was produced by Seth Boyden.

1820   According to the census report of the United States government, the population was 6,507.

July 28. The first issue of the New Jersey Eagle appeared.

1824   September 23. Marquis de Lafayette paid a visit to Newark.

1826   July 4. The process for producing malleable iron was invented by Seth Boyden.

November 13. St. John's Church, the first Roman Catholic house of worship, was organized on Mulberry Street.

1830   According to the census report of the United States government, the population was 10,953.

April 23. The first choral group, named the Harmonic Society of Newark, was organized, with Amos Holbrook as chairman.

1832   March 1. The first issue of the <u>Newark
            Daily Advertiser</u> appeared.

            March 7. The first railroad to serve Newark,
            The New Jersey Railroad and Transportation
            Company, was granted a charter by the New
            Jersey legislature, with operations of the
            line starting two years later.

1833   The number of dwellings was 1,542.

            June 14. President Andrew Jackson and Vice
            President Martin Van Buren paid a visit to
            Newark.

            November 20. Senator Henry Clay of Kentucky
            paid a visit to Newark, being well received
            in the industrially-oriented town because
            of his championing of the protective tar-
            iff.

1834   February 19. Clinton Township was formed in
            part from a portion of Newark.

1835   The town exported goods valued at more than
            $8 million.

            May 7. The Fourth Presbyterian Church, on
            Mulberry Street, was dedicated.

            October 27. A fire starting in a boarding
            house in the main section of the town burned
            out of control, destroying an entire block
            of buildings.

1836   Oil lamps were installed on the streets for
            illumination.

            March 18. Newark was incorporated as a city
            with a mayor and common council through the
            acceptance by a public vote of an act of in-
            corporation passed by the New Jersey legis-
            lature the preceding month.

            April 11. The first mayoral election was
            held, with attorney William Halsey chosen to
            fill the post.

            August 24. The cornerstone of the new city
            hall and court house building was laid, the
            structure being completed two years later.

1837   The number of slaves owned by residents was

twenty.

The fire department had seven engines stationed at various locations, including the
railroad depot and two churches.

October 2. Service was begun between Newark
and Madison on the Morris and Essex Railroad.

1838   The first high school was opened.

January 1. Service was begun between Newark
and Morristown on the Morris and Essex Railroad.

1840   According to the census report of the United
States government, the population was
17,290.

The number of slaves owned by residents was
three.

1842   January 31. The first mass at St. Mary's
Roman Catholic Church was celebrated.

1843   The first public school building was constructed.

1844   May 1. A leading citizen of Newark, attorney
Theodore Frelinghuysen, who had served as
United States senator from New Jersey from
1829 to 1835 and as mayor of Newark from
1837 to 1839, was nominated for vice president (with Henry Clay as the presidential
nominee) by the Whig Party at its convention
in Baltimore, Maryland.

August 23. An ordinance was passed creating
the post of city marshal and setting forth
its duties as well as those of the subsidiary
law enforcement officers.

October 28. Washington Hall was opened on
Broad Street, with a concert by vocal solo-
ists and an instrumental quartet.

1845   January 31. A bill of the New Jersey legislature was signed by Governor Daniel Haines
authorizing the founding of the Mutual Benefit Life Insurance Company.

February 27. The constitution of the New
Jersey Historical Society was adopted in

Trenton by the founders, who months later set up the organization's quarters in Newark.

1846   May 14. The first fire hydrants were supplied with water.

December 25. The Newark Gas Light Company began the production of gas for the gas lamps that had been newly installed on the streets for illumination.

1847   February 13. The Concert Hall (subsequently called the Newark Theatre), the first building constructed for professional theatrical performances, opened at Market and Halsey streets.

February 19. The Newark Library Association was granted a charter.

November 11. The recently organized choral group of German-speaking male residents, the Eintracht Männergesang Verein, presented its first concert.

1848   October 6. Congregation B'nai Jeshurun, the first synagogue, received its certificate of incorporation.

1849   July 27. The Lafayette Street Public School was opened.

1850   According to the census report of the United States government, the population was 38,894.

March 17. Saint Patrick's Roman Catholic Cathedral, at Washington Street and Central Avenue, was dedicated.

1851   February 17. The Newark Sacred Music Association was organized.

December 1. The Newark City National Bank opened for business.

1853   October 30. James Roosevelt Bayley was consecrated in St. Patrick's Cathedral, New York City, as the first bishop of the Diocese of Newark, which embraced the entire state of New Jersey.

1854   June 21. The Young Men's Catholic Association was organized.

1855   January 26. The board of education established the Normal School as a teacher training institution for the city.

May 31. The baseball club in Newark joined
with baseball clubs in four other communities
to form an intercity league.

June 2. The first performance of an opera
took place, with a production of Carl Maria
von Weber's "Der Freischütz" at the Newark
Theatre.

October 20. Congregation B'nai Abraham, the
second synagogue, filed a certificate of incorporation with the county authorities.

December 20. Service was begun between Newark and Bloomfield on the Newark and Bloomfield Railroad.

1857   May 28. Jacob Allen, the first member of
the fire department to be killed while on
duty, died while combatting a fire at the
Newark India Rubber Company building at Plane
and Halsey streets.

November 2. The first issue of the Newark
Evening Journal appeared.

December 23. A modern-type police department
was established.

1858   April 25. The first issue of the New Jersey
Freie Zeitung appeared.

1859   November 22. A United States government
patent was granted to James Jay Mapes for
the development of the first artificial fer-
tilizer twelve years earlier.

1860   According to the census report of the United
States government, the population was 71,941.

February 1. A leading citizen of Newark,
attorney William Pennington, who had served
as governor of New Jersey from 1837 to 1843,
was as a representative from New Jersey chosen speaker of the House of Representatives
for the Thirty-sixth Congress.

March 20. An act of the New Jersey legislature authorized the city officials to purchase the property of the Newark Aqueduct Company, a private water firm, for the purpose of establishing a public water company to supply residents with water.

June 17. The first system of public transportation went into operation with horse-drawn streetcars.

1861   February 21. Abraham Lincoln passed through the city on his way to Washington, D. C., where he was to be inaugurated the sixteenth president of the United States.

May 3. The first troops from Newark departed to fight for the Union in the Civil War.

1862   June 5. Service began between Newark and Orange on the horse-drawn car line.

1863   July 13. Soon after news of draft riots in New York City had been received, mobs protested President Abraham Lincoln's announcement that young men would be conscripted into military service to fight for the Union.

1864   June 2. The first police station, a three-story building on William Street (in the rear of the new city hall under construction), was completed.

September 24. The new city hall, at Broad and William streets, was opened.

1865   April 24. The funeral train bearing the body of the assassinated President Abraham Lincoln passed through the city on the way to Springfield, Illinois, for burial.

July 5. The Passaic Boat Club was organized.

1866   May 17. Newark celebrated the hundredth anniversary of its founding with a number of activities, including church services and a parade.

June 17. Saint James' Roman Catholic Church at Lafayette and Jefferson streets was dedicated.

July 4. The New Jersey Home for Disabled

Veterans, on Seventh Avenue, was opened.

1867   February 13. St. Barnabas Hospital was in-
         corporated.

1868   January 15. The New Jersey State Associa-
         tion of Baseball Players was organized in
         Newark.

         February 24. The Newark Board of Trade (the
         forerunner of the Chamber of Commerce of the
         City of Newark, which was subsequently re-
         named the Newark Association of Commerce and
         Industry, and then the Greater Newark Chamber
         of Commerce) was founded.

         May 10. The Children's Aid Society was or-
         ganized.

1869   May 14. The first issue of the <u>Newark Morn-
         ing Register</u> appeared.

1870   According to the census report of the United
         States government, the population was 105,059.

         February 19. An electric fire alarm system,
         totalling sixty alarm boxes, was installed.

         March 31. Inventor Seth Boyden died at the
         age of eighty-two.

         July 29. The first sheet asphalt pavement
         in the nation was laid on William Street.

1871   April 3. The Merchants National Bank was
         organized.

         May 8. St. Michael's Hospital was incor-
         porated.

         November 1. Author Stephen Crane, best
         known for his novel <u>The Red Badge of Courage</u>,
         was born in Newark.

1872   May 18. The first issue of <u>The Sunday Call</u>
         appeared.

         August 20. The Newark Industrial Exhibition
         was opened at the skating rink on Washington
         Street, making Newark the first city in the
         nation to hold an exhibit of its own wares.

1875   October 13. The Prudential Insurance Company

of America (initially named the Prudential
Friendly Society) was organized.

1876   September 30. The New Institute Hall on
Washington Street (the building had served
as the Newark Industrial Institute), opened
as a concert hall.

1877   December 26. The first national convention
of the Socialist Labor Party of North America
was held in Newark.

1878   January 13. The Young Men's Hebrew Association was founded.

September 3. The Institute Boat Club was
organized.

1880   Zccording to the census report of the United
States government, the population was 136,508.

April 29. The Little Sisters of the Poor was
incorporated.

December 28. Former President Ulysses S.
Grant and generals William T. Sherman
and George B. McClellan attended the un-
veiling of the statue of General Philip
Kearny in Military Park.

1881   January 20. The Newark Electric Light and
Power Company was incorporated.

March 25. Saint Benedict's College was
chartered.

December 19. A leading citizen of Newark,
attorney Frederick Theodore Frelinghuysen,
who had served as attorney general of New
Jersey from 1861 to 1866 and United States
senator from New Jersey from 1866 to 1869 and
from 1871 to 1877, was appointed secretary
of state by President Chester A. Arthur.

1884   February 12. The Roseville Athletic Association was founded.

1885   February 9. The Newark Technical School
(the forerunner of the Newark College of
Engineering) opened.

1887   March 23. The Newark District Telegraph Company was organized.

November 20. The North End Club was incorporated.

1889   May 25. The Hebrew Educational Society was organized.

October 17. The first free public library was opened in the Park Theatre building.

1890   According to the census report of the United States government, the population was 181,830.

February 1. The police department expanded its communications facilities with the introduction of a signal box system.

March 29. The city purchased a new plant for the distribution of water.

May 11. The First Baptist Peddie Memorial Church was dedicated.

May 13. The statue of inventor Seth Boyden was unveiled in Washington Park.

October 4. The first electrified trolley car service began with the operation of the Springfield Avenue line.

October 21. The board of health began the compilation of vital statistics with the recording of a recent death.

1892   December 13. The L. Bamberger & Co. department store opened for business.

1894   January 31. The Essex Lyceum opened as a concert hall.

1895   October 30. The second police precinct station was opened at Summer and Seventh avenues.

1898   May 2. The First Regiment of the New Jersey Volunteers organized to fight in the Spanish-American War departed from Newark. It returned from the Caribbean area the following September.

September 3. A United States government patent was granted to the Rev. Hannibal Williston Goodwin for both the invention of celluloid photographic film and the process for producing it twelve years earlier.

1899   January 26. The cornerstone of the Newark
            Public Library was laid.

            February 1. Barringer High School was o-
            pened.

            THE TWENTIETH CENTURY

1900   According to the census report of the United
            States government, the population was 246,070.

            February 27. A fire starting in a depart-
            ment store located in a section containing
            many dry goods establishments caused losses
            amounting to about $1 million and destroyed
            more than a score of buildings.

            May 24. Saint James Hospital was opened.

            September 23. The city acquired a new plant
            for the distribution of water.

            November 24. The site for the new city hall
            was selected on Broad Street.

1901   March 14. The Newark Public Library was
            opened.

            June 17. The City Trust Company opened for
            business.

            October 1. The Federal Trust Company opened
            for business.

1902   April 1. Politician and author Thomas Dunn
            English, best known for his poem "Ben Bolt,"
            who lived in Newark for the last twenty
            years of his life, died at the age of eighty-
            three.

            June 2. The West Side Trust Company opened
            for business.

1903   August 15. The cornerstone of the new city
            hall was laid.

            October 15. The Young Men's Christian Asso-
            ciation building, on Halsey Street, was ded-
            icated.

            December 20. The first ticket at the Lacka-
            wanna Railroad Station on Broad Street was

sold.

1904   May 30. A new police precinct station was
opened at Seventeenth Avenue and Livingstone
Street.

October 1. The first tax-supported business
library in the nation opened as a branch of
the Newark Public Library.

1905   March 22. The Newark Provident Loan Association was organized.

April 27. City officials announced the
start of an extensive campaign against mosquito infestation.

1906   December 20. The new city hall was dedicated.

1907   June 3. The Ironbound Trust Company opened
for business.

1908   January 9. The statue of Episcopal clergy-
man George H. Doane was unveiled near Trinity
Episcopal Church.

January 29. Beth Israel Hospital, at High
and West Kinney streets, was opened.

February 22. The first automobile show held
in the city took place in Electric Park.

October 5. The New Jersey Law School was
opened.

November 19. The American National Bank (initially named the American Commercial Bank)
opened for business.

1909   February 1. The Newark Anti-Tuberculosis
Association was established.

April 29. The Newark Museum Association was
incorporated by a group of citizens, including John Cotton Dana, librarian of the
Newark Public Library.

1910   According to the United States Bureau of the
Census, the population was 347,469.

February 23. The Clinton Trust Company o-
pened for business.

December 23. The first official fire prevention program was undertaken by the fire
department, with the issuance of a fire prevention code.

1911   January 3. The National Bank, at Broad and
Market streets, opened for business.

February 1. The Central Manual Training and
Commercial High School was opened.

May 30. The statue of Abraham Lincoln, seated
on a bench in front of the Essex County Court
House, by Gutzon Borglum was unveiled by former President Theodore Roosevelt.

December 20. Service began between Newark
and New York City on the Hudson and Manhattan
Railroad, using tunnel facilities under the
Hudson River which were soon to be familiarly
known as "The Tubes."

1912   March 4. The Springfield Avenue Trust Company opened for business.

October 30. A new police precinct station
was opened at Bigelow and Hunterdon streets.

November 2. The statue of George Washington
in Washington Park was unveiled. President
William H. Taft was prevented from being in
attendance because of the death of Vice
President James S. Sherman.

November 20. The Liberty Trust Company
opened for business.

1913   July 1. The New Jersey State Normal School
at Newark was established, having been con-
verted from the teacher training institution
for Newark alone into an institution for the
preparation of teachers for all communities
in the state of New Jersey.

September 2. The Young Women's Christian
Association building, on Washington Street,
was dedicated.

December 17. A new police precinct station
was opened on South Orange Avenue.

1914   February 1. The common council adopted a
resolution forbidding theatrical performances

on Sundays.

August 29. Plans were drafted for the construction of a $5 million terminal project by the Public Service Corporation.

September 14. The Newark Meadows Improvement Company was founded to reclaim the nearby meadowlands.

December 11. Boxing events were prohibited by the chief of police due to the number of serious injuries sustained by participants during the contests.

1915   June 19. The Ministerial Association was notified by Mayor Thomas L. Raymond that its position against the holding of amusement activities on Sundays would be considered by city officials.

October 20. Port Newark was opened.

1916   March 11. The board of health announced that there was an epidemic of measles.

March 28. During a strike for higher wages and shorter hours by the trolley car conductors and motormen's union, trolley cars run by nonunion personnel were stoned, causing the arrest of the union leaders.

May 1. The celebration of the two hundred fiftieth anniversary of the founding of Newark was formally opened with addresses by Mayor Thomas L. Raymond and New Jersey Governor James E. Fiedler at Proctor's Palace Theatre on Broad Street.

May 30. At one of the activities of the two hundred fiftieth anniversary of the founding of Newark, a historical pageant was presented to an audience of approximately forty thousand at Weequahic Park.

June 23. The city received greetings on the two hundred fiftieth anniversary of its founding from the officials of Newark-on-Trent, England, after which it was named.

1917   October 9. The commission form of government supplanted the mayor-council form by a three-to-one referendum vote.

October 17. Joseph C. McKinney was killed
in battle in World War I, the first of 443
servicemen from Newark to die in the conflict, in which a total of 20,876 from the
city served.

1918   May 27. The board of education voted to form
no new classes in German for the duration of
World War I and to institute loyalty tests
for public school teachers.

May 30. The Agawam, the first of one hundred
fifty war supply ships built at Port Newark,
was launched.

July 2. The city authorities were notified
by President Woodrow Wilson of his appreciation for the renaming of Hamburg Place to
Wilson Place, done as a result of anti-German
feeling.

August 1. In order to release men for military service, the police department appointed
its first three women.

November 11. The celebration of the signing
of the armistice ending World War I took
place in a variety of activities throughout
the city.

1919   May 20. On its return from Europe the United
States One Hundred Thirteenth Infantry of
the Twenty-ninth Division, composed in part
of the Newark-based First Infantry of the
New Jersey National Guard, was welcomed by
large crowds.

August 22. The Bureau of Child Hygiene announced a decrease in the birth rate of Newark, due, it was presumed, to large numbers
of men going into military service.

1920   According to the United States Bureau of the
Census, the population was 414,524.

October 26. Mayor Charles P. Gillen ordered
the flag at city hall to be flown at half-
staff in honor of Terence MacSwiney, Lord
Mayor of Cork, Ireland, who had died the preceding day in a hunger strike while imprisoned
for participating in the Irish independence
movement.

November 4. A proposal for the construction of a new power and light plant to serve the city was approved by a public vote.

December 9. A number of saloons were raided for operating in disregard of the newly passed Eighteenth (Prohibition) Amendment.

1921   May 21. A new police precinct district station was opened at Market and Read streets.

September 8. City officials issued bonds for the development of Newark Bay into a seaport.

October 5. The first baseball world series broadcast was presented by radio station WJZ, located in a hut on top of the Westinghouse Company plant in Newark, with coverage of the New York Giants-New York Yankees game finishing eight days later.

1922   January 26. A member of the board of education, J. M. Hauber, began a "crusade" against permitting girls in the public schools to attend classes wearing dresses short enough to expose their knees.

February 10. City officials announced they would take legal action against newsstand operators who sold "objectionable" magazines.

February 22. Radio station WOR presented its first broadcast from a room at the L. Bamberger & Son department store.

May 1. The bakers' union went on strike as a result of the bakery owners' refusing to accept a contract providing for an eight per cent wage increase.

October 1. The first international broadcast, transmitted from Newark to London, was presented by radio station WOR, with British tea merchant and yachtsman Sir Thomas Lipton participating.

October 7. The first chain broadcast was presented by radio stations WJZ and WGY, the latter located at the General Electric Company plant in Schenectady, New York, with the transmission of a baseball world series game from the Polo Grounds in New York City, where

a single microphone was connected to regular telephone lines leading to the two radio
stations.

1923   January 18. The Newark Athletic Club's build-
              ing was opened.

              April 21. The new Municipal Market building,
              acclaimed as the finest in the nation, was
              completed.

              August 8. Director of Public Safety William
              J. Brennan notified all fourteen of the cap-
              tains in the police department that the city
              must be rid soon of vices, particularly gamb-
              ling, or they would be suspended and placed
              of trial for dereliction of duty.

              December 9. The monument in Lincoln Park in
              memory of those who died in World War I was
              dedicated.

              December 31. The city commission approved a
              contract for the purchase of water from Mont-
              clair, New Jersey.

1924   September 29. The property tax rate in New-
              ark was announced by the New Jersey League
              of Municipalities to be the highest of those
              of the large cities of the state.

1925   April 16. The port of Newark was placed un-
              der the jurisdiction of the port of New York
              by order of President Calvin Coolidge so as
              to facilitate the administrative duties in-
              volved in the clearing of ships.

1926   February 16. Plans for the construction of
              a new Pennsylvania Railroad Station were out-
              lined by company president William W. Atter-
              bury.

              March 17. The Newark Museum, which had been
              housed since its founding fifteen years ear-
              lier in the upper levels of the Newark Pub-
              lic Library, opened its own $700,000 building
              on Washington Street, a gift of department
              store owner Louis Bamberger.

              March 27. In a federal government report
              Newark was listed in seventh place among the
              nation's cities in terms of current building
              construction.

May 31. "The Wars of America," a monument by Gutzon Borglum in Military Park in memory of those who fought in the Revolution, Civil War, Spanish-American War, and World War I, was dedicated by Secretary of the Navy Curtis D. Wilbur.

1927   January 22. *The Newark Evening News* announced plans for the construction of a new nine-story plant on Market Street.

April 18. The Mutual Benefit Life Insurance Company's new building, on Broadway, was opened.

August 6. Public buildings and the homes of city officials were placed under police guard as a precautionary measure against violence (the fear was subsequently proved groundless) by sympathizers of Nicola Sacco and Bartolomeo Vanzetti. They had been found guilty of murder in a Massachusetts court, but were believed by many to have been convicted because of their anarchist beliefs rather than by the evidence.

October 12. The statue of Christopher Columbus in Washington Park was unveiled.

December 25. The site for Newark Airport was selected by city officials.

1928   January 19. A $1.25 million annex to city hall, committed to the exclusive use of the board of education, was dedicated.

January 28. Port Newark was officially named "The Port of Newark" to end the confusion that led many to believe that Port Newark was a separate and distinct municipality.

May 16. *The New Jersey Freie Zeitung* purchased a site for the construction of a new two-story plant on Academy Street.

August 21. The city was sued by the Essex County Mosquito Extermination Commission for failing to drain adjacent marshes.

October 7. Mayor Thomas L. Raymond died in office of heart failure.

October 28. The Newark Airport was opened.

October 30. Plans to build the Fabian Theatre on Broad Street were announced by the Stanley Company.

November 15. Plans to erect a department store on Elizabeth Avenue were announced by Sears, Roebuck and Company.

November 26. Approximately $75,000 worth of opium was confiscated in a police raid on a residence on Mulberry Street.

1929   April 20. The first airplane commutation tickets in the nation were sold, inaugurated by American Airways at Newark Airport for the Newark-Boston line.

June 1. Newark Airport was designated as the eastern terminus for United States airmail service.

July 21. John Cotton Dana, noted head of the Newark Public Library and Newark Museum, died at the age of sixty-four.

July 22. The bus and trolley car operators demanded an eight-hour work day from their employer, the Public Service Corporation, a private gas, electric, and transportation firm.

August 23. A second annex to city hall was dedicated.

September 16. Department store owner Louis Bamberger distributed $1 million among 236 veteran employees for conscientious and loyal service.

December 1. The Newark Junior League announced plans for opening a day nursery for black children.

1930   According to the United States Bureau of the Census, the population was 442,337.

June 7. Department store owner Louis Bamberger and his sister, Mrs. Felix Fuld, announced a donation of $5 million for the establishment of the Institute for Advanced Study in Princeton, New Jersey.

July 5. The city began receiving water from

the Wanaque reservoir.

August 28. Hayes Park, West, became a part
of the city park system.

October 20. The police department reported
that jail cells of precinct stations were
being used for sleeping purposes by those
who were homeless because of the Depression.

1931   April 29. Boys served in various municipal
posts in observation of the Boys' Day Citi-
zenship project.

June 18. The city commission was upheld by
the United States Supreme Court in its decision to contribute municipal funds toward
a model tenement project under the auspices
of the Prudential Insurance Company of America, against a contention that such action
aided private enterprise and was therefore
unconstitutional.

October 22. The police department installed
teletype service in its headquarters in order to improve communication in its operations.

October 28. The New Jersey Historical Society held groundbreaking exercises for the
construction of its new building on Broadway.

1932   January 21. The chamber of commerce recommended that, because of the Depression, the
city commission reduce the salaries of municipal employees in order to lower the budget,
a recommendation opposed by Mayor Jerome T.
Congleton.

February 4. Municipal employees, through legal counsel, opposed any reduction in their
salaries and criticized the chamber of commerce for recommending that such an action
be taken in order to lower the budget.

February 21. A United States government patent was granted to William Nelson Goodwin,
Jr., of the Weston Electrical Instrument
Corporation of Newark for the invention of
the camera exposure meter a year earlier.

July 6. The city commission voted to reduce
the salaries of municipal employees from one

to fifteen per cent, limiting the measure
to the end of the following year, as a con-
cession to the employees.

August 25. Amelia Earhart, the first woman
to make a non-stop transcontinental flight
from Los Angeles, California, landed at
Newark Airport.

November 24. The Pulaski Skyway over the
nearby Passaic and Hackensack rivers was
completed.

1933   March 21. The first cross-country test of
instrument ("blind") flying was made by
James Kinney, who landed at Newark Airport
from College Park, Maryland.

March 25. The city met a defaulted March 16
payroll through an advanced collection of
taxes.

May 23. The city dismissed fifty-one employees as an economy measure.

June 2. The city dismissed forty employees
as an economy measure.

July 11. The city dismissed seventy-three
employees as an economy measure.

September 5. Weequahic High School was o-
pened.

November 6. The city commission adopted a
resolution that Newark would buy goods made
only under the NRA (National Recovery Administration) codes.

November 15. The city met a defaulted November 1 payroll through a loan from the
Public Service Corporation.

1934   February 27. The city received a loan from
the Prudential Insurance Company of America
to meet the upcoming March 1 payroll.

March 12. A petition was filed with the city
clerk calling for a referendum on the adoption of a city manager form of government
in place of the current commission form.
The city clerk rejected the document eleven
days later because it allegedly contained a

number of fraudulent signatures.

March 13. The city added $250,000 to its current budget to be used for relief purposes.

April 21. The cornerstone of the new post office building was laid.

August 1. The first transcontinental commercial overnight transport service was begun, with a flight from Newark Airport to Los Angeles, California.

October 3. The police department equipped its cars with shortwave radio sets.

1935   March 23. The new Pennsylvania Railroad Station was dedicated.

May 26. Service began on the underground trolley car line between Broad Street and Heller Parkway.

September 11. The Festival of Progress parade was held, celebrating what was considered to be a recent upswing in industry and trade.

December 2. The police department installed radio receiving sets in its headquarters to pick up alarms direct from New York City, Jersey City, New Jersey, and Bergen County, New Jersey.

1936   March 18. The city commission voted to restore to their original levels all salaries of municipal employees that had been reduced to lower the budget, but announced that reductions in the higher salaries might be subsequently imposed.

April 22. The city commission adopted an ordinance authorizing a $1 million bond issue for relief purposes.

1937   January 16. The first jury school in the nation was opened by a federal judge of the United States District Court for the district of New Jersey, located in Newark, to acquaint citizens with various aspects of courtroom procedure.

April 6. The first grand jury in the nation

to have a woman serve as foreman, the Federal Grand Jury in the United States District Court for the district of New Jersey, began its session at Newark.

December 2. Mayor Meyer C. Ellenstein and twenty-six other persons, including current and former city officials, were indicted on various charges of conspiracy to defraud the city and of dereliction of duty in land purchases by the city for the future development of the Port of Newark.

December 18. Trolley car service on Broad Street was ended.

1938 November 15. The indictments of Mayor Ellenstein and others in the land purchases fraud case were upheld by the New Jersey Supreme Court.

1939 April 23. A mistrial was declared in the land purchases fraud case, resulting from the defense counsel's refusal to continue with eleven jurors after one juror had been stricken with appendicitis.

1940 According to the United States Bureau of the Census, the population was 429,760.

January 6. Mayor Ellenstein and his co-defendants were acquitted in the retrial of the land purchases fraud case.

1941 December 8. In immediate response to the Japanese attack on Pearl Harbor, large numbers of men enlisted in the armed forces to fight in World War II, a conflict in which a total of 56,104 from the city served.

1942 September 29. A ring engaged in the stealing and sale of wartime gasoline ration coupons, which had threatened to undermine the gasoline allotment system in the city, was broken up by the police department.

December 4. The city's dismissal of public works department employees, who had gone on strike, on the ground that municipal employees have no right to strike, was upheld by the New Jersey Civil Service Commission.

1943 February 9. City officials announced that

several police stations and fire houses were without adequate heat because of wartime fuel oil shortages.

1945   March 26. The city commission offered a tax relief plan to the Prudential Insurance Company of America after the firm had declared that it might move because of what it considered to be an excessive tax burden.

May 8. The celebration of the surrender of Germany (V-E Day) ending the fighting in Europe in World War II took place in a variety of activities throughout the city.

August 14. The celebration of the surrender of Japan (V-J Day) ending World War II took place in a variety of activities throughout the city.

1946   July 1. A branch of Rutgers University, including the School of Law, was established in Newark, with the incorporation of the University of Newark, a private institution, into Rutgers University.

December 10. The Hotel Newarker was ordered closed on the ground that it had inadequate facilities for the prevention and containment of fire, as part of a move by the director of safety to have all hotels inspected for fire hazards.

1947   March 24. A bill to give the mayor of Newark greater control over the city's annual budget was approved by the New Jersey state assembly.

1949   May 13. Ralph A. Villani was chosen mayor after the post office impounded racially slanderous literature distributed by his opponent's supporters.

1950   According to the United States Bureau of the Census, the population was 438,176.

February 7. City officials sought the acquisition of a parcel of land owned by Elizabeth, New Jersey, as part of a site for a public housing project near the Newark-Elizabeth line.

1951   July 4. The American Civil Liberties Union

announced that it would ask the United States
Supreme Court to hear the case of an instruc-
tor dismissed from Newark College of Engineering for refusing to sign the New Jersey
anti-Communist loyalty oath, a case involving
the constitutionality of an oath directed at
teachers in public-supported schools.

July 25. The city commission approved plans
for a $10 million expansion of City Hospital.

1952   October 13. The $23 million Veterans Ad-
ministration Hospital at the Newark-Orange
line was dedicated.

October 15. Mail delivery service by helicopter between Newark and New York City was
begun.

December 23. In an unprecedented action,
Mayor Ralph A. Villani asked for the resignation of the entire membership of the board
of education alleging that it had been lax
in planning for new school buildings, whereupon six of the nine members issued a statement proclaiming their intention to remain
at their posts.

1953   January 25. A $1.5 million modernization
project of the Newark Public Library facilities was completed.

January 27. Freight service by helicopter
between Newark and New York City was begun.

February 5. A $1.5 million fund-raising cam-
paign for the Rutgers University School of
Law in Newark was launched.

February 18. The cornerstone of the new
Salvation Army building, at Washington
Street and Central Avenue, was laid.

April 28. The Newark Academy, a boys' pre-
paratory school, announced that it would
admit girls to the coming summer session,
the first time since 1859 that the institution would permit the attendance of female
students.

July 20. The new $8.5 million Newark Airport
terminal building was opened.

September 8. A new exchange, "TAlbot 8,"
was added to the eighteen exchanges serving
the city's approximately 214,000 telephones.

November 3. The mayor-council form of government supplanted the commission form by
a two-to-one referendum vote, held after the
Newark Charter Commission had issued a report declaring the commission type ineffi-
cient and recommending the change.

1954   May 11. Leo P. Carlin was elected mayor, the
first person chosen to fill the post through
a general election since 1915, when the city
adopted the commission form of government,
in which candidates were elected to the city
commission, which chose one of its members
to serve as mayor.

June 1. The new mayor-council form of government officially began to function.

October 19. The Cathedral of the Sacred
Heart was dedicated.

1955   April 25. The police department established
a new unit, the Youth Aid Bureau, to help
young people avoid involvement with crime.

May 24. In an action linked to recent hearings in the city by the House of Representatives Committee on Un-American Activities,
the city council voted unanimously to require all municipal employees to take a loyalty oath and to fill out a questionnaire on
affiliations with the Communist party and
other organizations listed as subversive by
the attorney general of the United States.

June 1. The New Jersey Council of the Congress of Industrial Organizations (CIO) and
the Americans for Democratic Action (ADA) ob-
jected to municipal employees having to sign
loyalty oaths and filling out questionnaires
on organizations listed as subversive.

June 11. Approximately five thousand municipal employees had submitted signed loyalty
oaths.

1956   August 25. City officials, civic organizations, and business firms (led by the Mutual
Benefit Insurance Company and the Prudential

Insurance Company of America) launched a
$100 million program to attract industry and
trade to rehabilitate the city.

1957 January 23. The first woman to serve as a
member of the city council, Mrs. Samuel E.
Cooper, was appointed to the post to fill
the vacancy caused by the death of her hus-
band.

February 16. Members of the police department were granted a forty-hour work week.

November 13. The Newark Housing Authority
voted to request from the federal Urban Renewal Administration a $12 million grant to
redevelop the Central Ward for light industry.

1958 March 17. Newark State College (the successor to the Normal School) moved from its
single building on one acre on Broadway to
its multi-building complex on a 120-acre
campus in Union, New Jersey.

September 27. City officials announced plans
for a redevelopment project on a ninety-acre
inner city site, which would include housing,
a cultural center, and an expansion of the
existing Rutgers University facilities.

1959 February 16. The New Jersey Supreme Court
upheld a Newark ordinance that required municipal employees to live within city limits,
affecting almost six hundred workers who resided elsewhere.

September 12. City officials announced plans
for a $191 million redevelopment project on
an inner city site, which would include middle income housing, office buildings, a shopping center, and a three-thousand-car garage.

October 3. City officials reveived plans
for a privately financed and operated
$95 million redevelopment project near the
Pennsylvania Railroad Station, which would
include apartment houses, a twenty-story office building, and another campus for the
South Orange, New Jersey-based Seton Hall
University.

December 3. The Newark Academy announced

plans to move to a new sixty-eight-acre campus in Livingston, New Jersey.

1960   According to the United States Bureau of the
Census, the population was 405,220, including
139,331 blacks who comprised 34.4 per cent
of the total.

January 12. The current mayor-council form
of government received a vote of confidence
over the previous commission form by a two-
to-one referendum vote.

April 13. The Real Estate Board of Newark,
Hillside, and Irvington recommended that
Newark Airport be expanded to accommodate
jet airplanes.

April 25. The police department appointed
its first meter maids.

September 14. The Prudential Insurance Company of America's new building, on Broad
Street, was dedicated.

1961   January 3. Mayor Leo P. Carlin announced the
formation of the Commitee for Small Business
Relocation Needs to offer guidance and
assistance to small business in areas
slated for redevelopment projects.

May 13. City officials requested a $150,000
federal grant to finance the study of the
development of 2,500 acres of nearby meadowlands for heavy industrial use.

1962   March 22. City officials received for their
consideration plans for a $232 million re-
development project on a 530-acre inner city
site, which would include middle and upper
income housing, office buildings, a shopping
center, hotels, and an industrial complex,
bringing to twelve the number of redevelopment projects in various stages of study by
the city.

May 8. Representative Hugh J. Addonizio was
elected mayor after a campaign noted for its
acrimony, defeating incumbent Carlin by a
two-to-one vote.

July 2. Chosen president of the board of
education was Verner V. Henry, the first

black to fill that post in the body, which
included a newly appointed black, Harold
Ashby, making this the first time that two
blacks had served together on the board.

July 18. The Newark Housing Authority received from the federal Urban Renewal Administration a $7.7 million grant to acquire
and clear land for two downtown redevelopment projects: the construction of the Colonnade Apartments, which would be a middle
income housing complex, and the rehabilita-
tion of the campuses of Newark College of
Engineering, Rutgers University, and Seton
Hall University.

November 24. Nine black patrolmen were promoted by the police department to the position of detective, the largest number of
black officers to be so promoted at one
time.

1963   April 6. Mayor Addonizio rejected a demand
by interracial groups for the establishment
of a citizens' review board to investigate
charges of police brutality, but added that
he planned to form citizen groups to promote
a better relationship between police officers
and the public.

July 18. The police department established
the Human Relations Board to assist in pro-
moting better understanding between police
officers and the public.

1964   March 30. Members of a civil rights group
began a sit-in at city hall to protest a
projected increase in the property tax rate,
contending that blacks would bear the brunt
of the rise.

June 26. City officials created a special
police group to protect public housing projects.

November 21. The Newark Housing Authority
received from the federal Urban Renewal Administration a $37 million grant to acquire
and clear land for redevelopment projects in
the St. Michael's Hospital area on South
Broad Street and in the Central Ward.

December 23. The Neighborhood Youth Corps

was established, the first of such projects
under the federal government's new antipoverty program in which young persons would
be employed in a variety of city jobs, such
as clerical assistant, engineer's helper, and
manual laborer.

1965   June 19. The American Jewish Congress and
the National Urban League established a program to offer guidance and assistance to
black businessmen and black students seeking
a career in business, administered by an
organization named the Greater Newark Interracial Council for Business Opportunity and
headed by former New Jersey Governor Robert
B. Meyner.

June 30. City officials proposed to the
federal Office of Economic Opportunity and
to the United Community Corporation, the
Essex County arm of Newark's antipoverty
effort, five new antipoverty projects, at a
total estimated cost of $1.5 million.

September 15. Mayor Addonizio rejected the
demand for the establishment of a citizens'
review board, but announced that he would
request the Federal Bureau of Investigation
to examine cases of alleged police brutality,
an action which the president of the Newark
Patrolman's Benevolent Association commended.

1966   January 1. In connection with the upcoming
celebration of the three hundredth anniversary of the founding of Newark, city officials received a congratulatory message from
President Lyndon B. Johnson praising Newark's
accomplishments.

January 7. The Ku Klux Klan announced that
it would make efforts to recruit members
from the police department, prompting the
police director to declare that any member
of the force who joined the Klan would be
dismissed, in accordance with department
regulations regarding affiliation with organizations listed as subversive by the attorney general of the United States.

February 14. The city received from the federal government a $6.8 million grant to fi-
nance new antipoverty projects designed to
increase the employability of large numbers

of jobless persons, most of them young, by
raising the level of their basic education
and their occupational skills.

May 18. The celebration of the three hundredth anniversary of the founding of Newark
took place, with a lavish parade down Broad
Street, attended by the mayor of Newark-on-
Trent, England, after which the city was
named, and observed by a crowd estimated at
250,000.

June 14. Mayor Addonizio was elected to a
second term in a run-off contest, defeating
former Mayor Leo P. Carlin by a more than
two-to-one vote.

1967   According to the migration division of the
Commonwealth of Puerto Rico, there were in
the city approximately twenty-six thousand
Puerto Ricans, including those born in Puerto
Rico and those born in the United States of
Puerto Rican parents.

July 13. Violence erupted, apparently set
off by the resentment of a crowd of blacks
gathering to protest the arrest of a black
cab driver on charges of assaulting a white
policeman. The disorders, in which bands of
persons smashed windows, looted stores, and
stoned policemen, centered around the fourth
police precinct station. Lasting six days,
the rioting resulted in twenty-three deaths,
approximately 1,200 injuries, approximately
1,300 arrests, and over $10 million in pro-
perty damage.

July 21. At the National Conference on
Black Power, held in Newark and attended by
representatives from organizations such as
the National Association for the Advancement
of Colored People, the National Urban League,
the Congress of Racial Equality, the Southern
Christian Leadership Conference, and the
Student Nonviolent Coordinating Committee,
a spokesman for the Congress of Racial Equality declared that his organization planned
to collect 25,000 signatures in the city demanding the resignation of Mayor Addonizio
for insensitivity to the needs of blacks.

July 23. Black poet-playwright LeRoi Jones
(later to become a black nationalist leader

known as Imamu Amiri Baraka), residing in
the city, charged the police department,
which he characterized as corrupt and racist,
with more than fifty cases of brutality
and "wanton murder" during the recent rioting
by blacks.

August 1. The Prudential Life Insurance Company of America announced it would provide
an $18 million long-term loan for a $24 mil-
lion redevelopment project, which would include a thirty-story office building, a ten-
story motel, an underground garage, and a
theater, near the Pennsylvania Railroad Station as part of an approximately $100 mil-
lion program to rehabilitate the downtown
section.

August 16. New York City Mayor John V. Lindsay toured the riot-struck areas of the city
in his capacity of vice chairman of President Lyndon B. Johnson's Advisory Commission
on Civil Disorders.

August 24. Charging that the police had deliberately destroyed black-owned property
during the recent riots, eighteen blacks
filed suit (based on an 1871 civil rights
law) in the United States District Court for
the district of New Jersey requesting the
federal government to take over the police
department on the ground that the police
consistently discriminated against blacks.

December 9. In a survey sponsored by the
Newark Office of Economic Development and
conducted by Rutgers University, it was
found that Spanish-speaking residents had
replaced blacks as the fastest-growing group
in the population.

1968   February 10. The Governor's Select Commission on Civil Disorder, a body appointed by
New Jersey Governor Richard J. Hughes to
study the 1967 riots, reported that both
blacks and whites in Newark sensed a "per-
vasive feeling of corruption at City Hall,"
and scored the attitude toward minority
groups of the entire city administration, particularly that of Mayor Addonizio and the
police department.

June 21. An all-black political convention

to seek consensus among blacks for the coming municipal elections was opened, sponsored by the newly formed United Brothers of Newark.

June 29. Work began on an office building, motel, and shopping mall, the first step in a redevelopment project near the Pennsylvania Railroad Station, which was part of a $100 million program to rehabilitate the downtown section.

July 20. The United States Office of Economic Development reported that almost $1.2 billion must be expended over the next decade to stem "blight and despair" and to raise Newark to the level of an "average city."

August 18. New Jersey state officials announced they would recruit almost one hundred blacks and Puerto Ricans who were interested in applying for the Newark police department, and provide them with part-time jobs while they prepared for the civil service examinations for the department.

1969   March 11. Reversing a position taken the preceding month that funds to the Newark Public Library and the Newark Museum be cut off because of financial difficulty, the city council voted to restore funds to both institutions for at least nine months, a move that was widely considered as one drawing attention to the need for more state aid.

August 6. New Jersey Governor Richard J. Hughes signed an act permitting the use of urban aid funds for increasing the salaries of policemen and firemen, a move that was expected to help Newark, where members of the police department and the fire department had been threatening a work stoppage if their pay were not raised.

October 6. Mayor Addonizio threatened legal action against Citizens for Lindsay for sponsoring a television commercial showing Newark as a victim of decay and riot-damage (containing visual materials on Newark which Addonizio maintained were not of damage but of redevelopment sites), implying that such would happen to New York City if John V. Lindsay were not re-elected mayor.

December 17. Mayor Addonizio, along with
fourteen other persons, including current
and former city officials, was indicted by
a federal grand jury on a charge of conspir-
ing to extort money from contractors doing
business with the city.

1970

According to the census report of the United
States government, the population was 381,930,
including 207,458 blacks, who comprised 54.3
per cent of the total and 27,443 of Puerto
Rican background, who comprised 7.2 per cent
of the total.

June 2. The trial began of Mayor Addonizio
and others charged with conspiracy in city
contract extortions.

June 16. Civil engineer Kenneth A. Gibson
was elected mayor, the first black chosen
chief executive of a major eastern seaboard
city, by defeating incumbent Addonizio in a
run-off election.

July 19. The Young Lords, a militant Puerto
Rican group, clashed with the police at the
city hall reviewing stand during the annual
Puerto Rican Day parade. The incident apparently started when a youth threw an effi-
gy of the governor of Puerto Rico at the
stand.

August 25. Princeton University established
a program in which a small group of under-
graduate students would live in Newark for a
semester and work on urban problems.

September 22. Having been found guilty two
months earlier, along with four others, of
conspiracy and extortion, former Mayor Addonizio was sentenced by a federal court to
serve ten years in prison and to pay a
$25,000 fine.

October 1. In a newspaper interview New
Jersey Governor William T. Cahill expressed
the hope that the federal government would
select Newark as a testing ground for whether
a deteriorating inner city can be saved.

DOCUMENTS

THE BILL OF SALE OF LAND TO THE FOUNDERS -- 1667

>The bill of sale of land by the
>local Indians to the founders of
>Newark, executed in July 1667,
>follows.

Source: East Jersey Records, Book 1, folio 9.

Know all men By these presents, that WEE, Wapamuc the Sakamaker, and Wamesane, Peter, Captamin, Wecaprokikan, Napeam, Perawae, Sessom, Mamustome, Cacanakque, and Hairish, Indians belonging now to Hakinsack, the known acknowledged proprietors of a certain tract of Land Lying on the West of Pesayak river being parties on the one Side, and Mr. Obediah Bruen, Mr. Samuel Kitchell, Michael Tomkins, John Browne, and Robert Denison, with the consent and advice of Capt'n Philip Carteret Governeur of the Province of New Jersey, and in the behalf of ye Inhabitants now being or to be ye possessors of the Tract of Land Inserted in this Deed of Sale the other parties, Doe make this Indenture the eleventh day of July in the year of our Lord 1667 (being the enlarging and perfecting of a deed of Sale made With the Indians the year before the present) in manner and form following, viz:
  THAT WEE, the said Wapamuck, the Sakamaker, and Wamesane, Peter, Captamin, Wecaprokikan, Napeam, Perawae, Sessom, Mamustome, Cacanakque, and Hairish, doe, for ourselves and With Consent of the Indians, Bargain, sell and deliver, a Certain tract of Land, Upland, and Meadows of all sorts, Wether Swamps, Rivers, Brooks, Springs, fishings, Trees of all sorts, Quaries, and Mines, or Metals of what sort soever, With full liberty of hunting for the above said proprietors that were uppon the upper commons, and of fishing in the above said Pesayak River; which said tract of land is bounded and Limited with the with the bay Eastward, and the great River Pesayak Northward, the great Creke or River in the meadow running to the head of the Cove, and from thence bareing a West Line for the South bounds, wh. said Great Creke is Commonly Called and known by the name Weequachick, on the West Line backwards in the Country to the foot of the great mountaine called Watchung, being as is Judged about seven or Eight miles from Pesayak towne; the said Mountaine as Wee are Informed hath one branch of Elizabeth towne River running near the above said foot of the mountaine; the bounds northerly, viz. Pesayak River reaches to the Third River above the towne, ye River is called Yauntakah, and from thence upon a northwest line to the aforesaid mountaine; all which before mentioned Lands for the several kinds of them, and all the singular benefits and Priviledges belonging to them, with ye several bounds affixed

and expressed herein, as also free liberty and range for
Cattle, horses, hoggs, and that though they Range beyond
any of the bounds in this deed Expressed, to feed and
pasture Without Molestation of or damage to the owners
of the cattle &c. above said. WEE the above said Indians,
Wapamuk, &c. doe sell, Alienate, make over and Confirm
all our Right, Title and Interest of us, our heires, and
Successors forever Unto the said Lands, &c. as above
mentioned to Mr. Obediah Bruen, Mr. Samuel Kitchell, Michael Tomkins, John Browne and Robert Denison, townsmen
and Agents for ye English Inhabitants of Pesayak, to them,
their heires and associates for Ever, to have, hold, and
dispose of, Without Claim, Let or Molestation from ourselves or any other Whatsoever. These Lands, &c. are
thus solde and delivered for and in consideration of fifty double-hands of powder, one hundred barrs of lead,
twenty Axes, twenty Coates, ten Guns, twenty pistolls,
ten kettles, ten Swords, four Blankets, four barrells of
beere, ten paire of breeches, fifty knives, twenty howes,
eight hundred and fifty fathem of wampem, two Ankors of
Licquers or something Equivolent, and three troopers
Coates; these things are received, only a small remainder
Engaged to them by bill. To the true and just performance according to ye true intent of our Bargain, WEE ye
said Obediah Bruen, and the rest above said, doe for
ourselves and heires, Ex'tors, Adm'n'tors or Assigns, to
the said Wapamuk, &c., the true proprietors of the said
Lands doe bind and Covenant. WEE the said Wapamuk and
the rest of the Indians above said doe fully surrender,
pas over and Yeild up all our Right, privilege and power
in the same, and to free the above said Lands from Claim,
Incumbrances, of What kind soever; all the above mentioned purchasse Wee doe Grant and deliver to Obediah
Bruen and ye rest above said, to them, their associates,
heires, and all the lawfull possessors. And for the
full Ratiffication and testification of the above said
bargain and agreements about the aforesaid tract and
parcells of Land so bounded, Wee, the said parties above
mentioned have hereunto Enterchangeably sett our hands
and seales, the day and year above said, in the presence
of Us Witnessing. Moreover Wee doe grant them free liberty to take what timber and stones they please in any
of our Lands, where Wee the above said Indians have yet
propriety.

HIRING A TEACHER -- 1676

On February 7, 1676, the residents
at a town meeting made arrangements to hire a teacher for the
young.

Source: <u>Records of the Town of Newark, New Jersey</u>, Newark, 1864, p. 67.

Item -- The Town hath consented that the Town's Men
should perfect the Bargain with the School Master for
this Year, upon Condition that he will come for this
Year, and do his faithful, honest, and true Endeavor,
to teach the Children or servants of those as have subscribed, the reading and writing of English, and also
Arethmetick if they desire it; as much as they are capable to learn and he capable to teach them, within the
Compass of this Year--nowise hindring but that he may
make what bargain he please, with those as have not
subscribed. It is voted that the Town's Men have Liberty
to compleat the Bargain with the School Master, they
knowing the Town's Mind.

A SMALLPOX THREAT -- 1679

On February 12, 1679, the residents
at a town meeting took measures a-
gainst the spread to their community of a smallpox epidemic in New
York.

Source: <u>Records of the Town of Newark, New Jersey</u>, Newark, 1864, p. 73.

Item--Upon a Report that many are sick of the Pox at
New York--It is thought fit to prohibit persons from
frequent going thither upon every small occasion, as
formerly. The Town hath therefore chosen as a Committee,
Mr. Ward, Mr. Johnson, Mr. Swain, Deacon Lawrence, and
Sarj't Harrison, to whom Persons shall repair for Liberty; and this Committee or any Three of them to consider
whether Persons occasions are of urgent Necessity, and
as they find, to give Liberty or Prohibit.
    Item--If any Person or Persons shall presume to go
without approbation from some of these Three, shall for-
feit the sum of 20 s. to be distrained by the Constable.

THE ESTABLISHMENT OF A SECURITY SYSTEM
1679

> On June 10, 1679, the residents at
> a town meeting established a secur-
> ity system.

Source: <u>Records of the Town of Newark, New Jersey</u>, Newark, 1864, p. 75.

For the better Security of the Town, it is agreed
to have a Watch kept in the Town, Three in a Night, at
some House appointed by the Sarjents, and one of the
Three to stand Centry, one at one Time and another at
another; and at break of Day or thereabouts all Three
of them to be walking, that if there be Danger it may
be timely discovered and prevented, and about half an
hour after Daybreak to call the Drummer, and he is to
beat the Drum. It is also agreed that one fourth Part
of the Town at a time, and so taking their Turns, shall
carry arms to Meeting on the Lord's Days--and two to
Ward and one to stand Centry.

A STAND AGAINST IRREVERENT BEHAVIOR -- 1680

On November 29, 1680, the residents
at a town meeting took a formal position against what was then regarded as irreverent behavior.

Source: <u>Records of the Town of Newark, New Jersey</u>, Newark, 1864, p. 80.

It is agreed upon by Vote, that a Man should be
chosen to look after and see that the Boys and Youth do
carry themselves reverently in the time of public Worship. And if any grown Persons shall carry themselves
irreverently, he is to make Complaint to the Authority
and present their Names; and his Word shall be accounted
Evidence against him or them offending, whether the
offence be committed within or without the House. Joseph
Walters is chosen to be the Man for the purpose above
said.

HIRING A MINISTER -- 1692

On August 23, 1692, the residents
at a town meeting decided to ask
a minister to lead their congregation.

Source: Records of the Town of Newark, New Jersey, Newark, 1864, p. 105.

It was consulted, consented, and unanimously agreed,
that Mr. John Pruden should be called to be their Minister; and in Case he should come and settle among them
in that Work, they would freely and readily submit themselves to him and to his Dispensations and Administra-
tions, from Time to Time in the Discharge of his ministerial Office and Works, as God shall assist and direct
him therein by his Word and Spirit, for their Spiritual
Good and Edification. It is also consulted, voted, consented to, and agreed by the said Inhabitants then convened, for Mr. John Pruden's Encouragement to come and
settle among them, and that he may the better attend upon the Work of the Ministry as his Business, and for the
more comfortable Sustanance of his Family in his Attendance therein; that he shall have £50 p. annum, and his
Fire Wood free: to be paid yearly, according to several
Contributions voluntarily subscribed by them, to Mr.
Pruden or his Order, so long as he shall continue with
them employed in the Ministry: this also voted.
It is moreover voted and agreed, that Mr. Pruden
shall have and hold such a Propriatie, and other Con-
veniences for his Accommodations in the Town, as shall be
agreed upon between him and the Committee appointed to
treat with him (viz) Mr. Ward, Mr. Johnson, John Curtis,
Azariah Crane, Jasper Crane, Thomas Ludington, and Stephen Bond, nominated and impowered by the Town for that
Purpose.

THE BOUNDARIES OF NEWARK -- 1713

A declaration regarding the boundaries of Newark made by the sur-
veyor in November, 1713, follows.

Source: <u>East Jersey Records</u>, Book A.A.A., folio 155.

By Warrant from His Excelencie ye Governeur, to me
Directed, bearing Date ye 7th Day of November, 1713.
Sirveyed, Marked out, & Acertained ye Lines and
Boundaries of ye Township of Newarke, According to their
Pattent or Charter, which bears Date ye 27th Day of Ap-
reill 1713: beginning where Bound Creek Emtieth itself
into Hackingsack Bay and Runing up ye s'd Creek to ye
head thereof, where a black Cherry tree Markd with ye
Letters N on the one Side & E on the other Stands under
a Steep hill, thence South Twenty one Degrees West Twenty
five Chaines forty Three Links to a Dead Black oak Tree,
Standing in Joseph Lyons feild, thence North Sixty Degrees fifteen Minutes West four Hundered and five Chain
or five Mile & five Chains along Markd Trees, many of
them being Markd with ye Letters N & E as aforesd (because tis ye Partition Line betwen Sd Newark & Elizabeth
Town) to a Black oak tree & a Small Red oak Tree by it,
both Markd on four Sides Standing on ye Riseing Ground of
ye South End of ye Mountain Call'd Watchung & about forty or fifty Rod North Easterly from ye Westmost of ye
Two branches of Raway River which Comes Down on Each Side
of ye s'd Mountain, Thence Extending on a Northerly
Course along ye Ridge of ye s'd Mountain to a heap of
Stones, Erected to Ascertain ye Boundaries between s'd
Town of Newark & the Town of Acquackanong, Thence on a
South East Course to ye brook or Rivollet Called ye
Third River, Where it falls into Pasayack River, Thence
Continuing Down ye s'd Pasayack River & Hackingsack Bay
to where it began.

By JOHN REID, Sirveyor.
A True Copy of ye Return of ye Sirvey of ye Township of Newark, Entered pr me.

JOHN COOPER, Town Clerk.

CHURCH CARE AND CEMETERY USE -- 1738

> On March 14, 1738, the residents
> at a town meeting made their an-
> nual arragements for the care of
> the Meeting House (church) and
> for the use of the cemetery for
> pasturing flocks.

Source: <u>Records of the Town of Newark, New Jersey</u>, Newark, 1864, p. 133.

. . . Samuel Alling and John Crane was appointed to
order the ringing of the Bell and Sweeping the Meeting
House, also to take Care of the burying Yard fence--it
was also voted that Hanah Shingelton should sweep the
Meeting House, provided she sweeps it clean and for the
same Wages as it was done for last Year. The feed of
the burying Place was sold to Isaac Lyon for the ensuing
Year, for the sim of Ł2 11s. 8d., to be put to the
same Use as it was last Year.

RULES FOR THE USE OF THE MINISTER'S LAND
1743

On March 8, 1743, the residents
at a town meeting established
rules regarding the use of the
land appropriated by the community for its minister.

Source: <u>Records of the Town of Newark, New Jersey</u>, Newark, 1864, pp. 135-136.

. . . it was voted, that any Person should be fined
20s. one half to the Complainer and the other half for
the Use of the Poor--that cuts any Tree or Trees, Spires
or Hoop-Poles upon any Part of the Parsonage, except
so much as is necessary for diging or carrying of any
Stones any Person may want for building or other Uses.
Nathaniel Wheeler, Nathaniel Johnson and Nathaniel Camp,
were chosen to run out the Parsonage Meadow, and to pro-
secute Trespassers on the same in the Trustees Name.

A LIVESTOCK MARKET -- 1768

An announcement made on August 16,
1768, regarding the buying and
selling of livestock follows.

Source: Frank J. Urquhart, <u>A History of the City of Newark, New Jersey</u>, New York, 1913, vol. I, pp. 237-238.

Whereas many inconveniences frequently attend the
sale of horses, horn cattle, sheep and swine, for want
of some publick convenient stated market or fair, where
sellers and buyers may meet for that purpose. And as
the town of Newark, from its vicinity to New York and
other circumstances attending its situation is by many
esteemed a most proper place for such a cattle market:
It is at the request of the Inhabitants of New York and
New Jersey that publick notice is hereby given, that on
the Third Wednesday in October next and on the Thursday
and Friday following, and on the same days yearly, and
every year thereafter, will be opened and held at Newark
aforesaid, a publick market for the sale of all kind of
horses, fat and store horn cattle, sheep, swine, and
for other purposes whatsoever (except it be for the sale
of the products or manufacturies of the country). Proper officers will attend for the preservation of decorum
and good order.

SUPPORTING THE COLONIAL CAUSE -- 1775

In May 1775 the residents gave formal support to the colonial cause
against Great Britain.

Source: American Archives, Fourth Series, Washington,
D. C., 1839, vol. II, p. 505.

At a meeting of the Freeholders and Inhabitants of
the Township of Newark, in New-Jersey, on Thursday, the
4th day of May, A. D. 1775:
DOCTOR WILLIAM BURNETT in the Chair.

An Association having been entered into and subscribed by the Freeholders and other Inhabitants of said
Town, a motion was made and agreed to, that the same be
read. The same was accordingly read and is as follows:
"We, the Freeholders and Inhabitants of the Township of Newark, having deliberately considered the open-
ly avowed design of the Ministry of Great Britain to
raise a revenue in America; being affected with horrour
at the bloody scene now acting in the Massachusetts-Bay
for carrying that arbitrary design into execution; firmly
convinced that the very existence of the rights and liberties of America can, under God, subsist on no other
basis than the most animated and perfect union of its inhabitants; and being sensible of the necessity, in the
present exigency, of preserving good order, and a due reg-
ulation in all publick measures, with hearts perfectly
abhorrent of slavery, do solemnly, under all the sacred
ties of religion, honour, and love to our Country, associate and resolve, that we will, personally, and as far
as our influence can extend, endeavour to support and
carry into execution whatever measures may be recommended
by the Continental Congress, or agreed upon by the proposed Convention of Deputies of this Province, for the
purposes of preserving and fixing our Constitution on a
permanent basis, and opposing the execution of the several despotick and oppressive Acts of the British Par-
liament, until the wished-for reconciliation between
Great Britain and America, on constitutional principles,
can be obtained.
"That a General Committee be chosen by this Town for
the purposes aforesaid, and that we will be directed by,
and support them in all things respecting the 'common
cause, the preservation of peace, good order, the safety
of individuals, and private property.'"
Voted, That Isaac Ogden, Esquire, Captain Philip
Van Cortlandt, Bethuel Pierson, and Caleb Camp, be the
Deputies to represent said Township in the Provincial
Congress referred to in the said Association.

The General Committee also mentioned in the said Association, was then chosen, consisting of forty-four.

Agreed, That the powers delegated to the Deputies and General Committee, continue until the expiration of five weeks after the rising of the next Continental Congress, and no longer.

Agreed, That the General Committee have power to appoint one or more Sub-Committees, to act on any emergency.   ISAAC LONGWORTH, Town Clerk.

The General Committee immediately convened, and elected Lewis Ogden, Esquire, Chairman, Doctor William Burnett, Deputy Chairman, and Elisha Boudinot, Esq., Clerk of the said General Committee.

Agreed, That the above-named Lewis Ogden, Esquire, Doctor William Burnett, Elisha Boudinot, Esquire, Isaac Ogden, Esquire, and Mr. Isaac Longworth, be a Committee of Correspondence for said Town.

Elisha Boudinot, Clerk to Committee.

RESOLUTIONS OF THE FIRE ASSOCIATION
1797

> The set of resolutions adopted by
> the Fire Association, the first
> corps of fire-fighters, which was
> established on January 26, 1797,
> follows.

Source: William H. Shaw, History of Essex and Hudson
Counties, New Jersey, Philadelphia, 1884, vol. I, pp.
458-459.

Resolved, That the subscription for the purpose of
raising money for the purchasing of fire-engines, so far
as respects the members of this association, be done a-
way with, and that no subscriber thereto, who is now or
may be an associator prior to the first assessment, shall
be held answerable to pay the sum he there subscribed,
but that each associator shall be considered liable to
be assessed, and to pay such sum or sums of money as the
assessors, agreeable to the principles of assessment,
. . . shall levy upon him.

Resolved, That three fire-engines be purchased for
the use of this association, under the direction of the
standing committee, of such powers and capacities as to
them shall appear most advisable, provided that the price
of one shall not exceed 150s. and the other two 180s.
each.

Resolved, That the sum of one thousand dollars be
raised to aid in carrying into effect the purposes of
this association.

Resolved, That the standing committee do immediately
purchase, at the expense of the association, such number
of fire-hooks, axes, ladders and other implements as they
shall judge necessary to render the effects of fire less
destructive.

Resolved, That the standing committee take in
charge the article of association and give the same a
general circulation through the town as soon as expedient,
and when done, that they deliver it to the assessors,
that they may proceed to execute the duties of their
office.

PRINCIPLES OF THE VOLUNTARY ASSOCIATION OF THE PEOPLE OF NEWARK TO OBSERVE THE SABBATH
1798

The statement of principle adopted
by the Voluntary Association of
the People of Newark to Observe
the Sabbath, which was established
on July 10, 1798, follows.

Source: Joseph Atkinson, <u>The History of Newark, New Jersey</u>, Newark, 1878, p. 172.

It being at all times proper for those who acknowledge themselves dependent creatures on the Supreme Being, and who call themselves Christians, to reflect upon their ways and reform whatever they think is contrary to the word of God; but more especially when the judgments of God are abroad in the world, and appear with a menacing aspect on our own County--And as the sanctity of the Sabbath is generally acknowledged by all Christians; and the experience of ages teaches, that whenever vice, like a flood, deluges a land, it commonly breaks in with a destruction of the holiness of that day, the observance of which seems to be daily lessening in this Country, to prevent which dreadful calamity--We, the subscribers, Inhabitants of Newark in New Jersey, deeply impressed with the importance of the religious Importance of the Sabbath, not only to the existence of our holy religion, but to the happiness of our Country--do associate and agree as follows:

1--That we will neither give nor partake of parties of pleasure or entertainments on that day.

2--That we will neither ride out nor travel (except in cases of necessity) on that day.

3--That we will regularly attend divine worship on that day, and compel our children, apprentices and servants to do the same as far as in our power lies--

4--That after divine service is over we will keep our children, apprentices and servants at home and not suffer them to go abroad on that day.

5--That we will exert ourselves to suppress all manner of employment and worldly business on the Sabbath.

6--That we will exert ourselves to assist and support the officers of Justice to put the laws in force against those who shall violate them on that day--and we will appoint a Committee from time to time of at least seven persons to assist the officers in carrying these Resolutions into effect--

7--That we will also extend our exertions to support the magistrates and officers of Justice to prevent all the immoralities and vices pointed out in the law for preventing vice and immorality.

THE PROTECTION OF SHEEP -- 1808

An act passed at a town meeting on
April 11, 1808, for the protection
of sheep in the community follows.

Source: Records of the Town of Newark, New Jersey, Newark, 1864, pp. 195-196.

Whereas the Legislature of this State by a Law
passed on the thirteenth day of March Eighteen hundred
and Six, did authorize the Inhabitants of the several
Townships at their Annual Town Meetings to order to be
levied, Assessed and Collected, such tax on Dogs, in addition to the Tax already imposed by Law--and to make
such other by laws as a Majority of each Town Meeting
may deem expedient for the protection of their Sheep.
Therefore 1st be it enacted by the Inhabitants of
the Township of Newark in the County of Essex, that the
Assessors of this Township shall at the Time of Assessing
the other taxes for the use of the Township, County, or
State, assess every Master or Mistress of any family in
which a Dog or Dogs of six months old and upwards are
kept whether by themselves or any Child, Servant or other
person whomsoever, the following sums of money, viz: If
only one Dog is kept by one family, One Dollar. If two
Dogs are so kept, five dollars and for every Dog so kept
above two, the further sum of twenty dollars, which Tax
shall be construed to include the Tax heretofore authorized by law, and shall be collected at the same time and
in the same manner in every respect, with the other Taxes
raised in the Township, except that the Assessor and Collector shall be each intitled to six cents for every Dog
returned in the Duplicate agreeably to this Act.
2d. And be it enacted, that if any person shall deny
that he or she have any property in any Dog so assessed
in his or her name, or shall refuse to give a fair account
of the number or age of the Dog or Dogs to remain about
his or her house, he or she shall be deemed to be the
owner of such Dog or Dogs and be liable to the payment of
the Tax aforesaid, and moreover shall be liable to a fine
of ten dollars for every Dog so harboured and not returned
to the Assessor when by him required, to be recovered before any Justice of the peace in this Township by the
Collector of the same, and to be applyed as is herein after directed.
3d. And be it enacted, that the amount of the said
Tax after deducting the charges of Assessing and Collecting the same and all fines which shall be recovered by
virtue of this Act, shall be appropriated, exclusively to
making good any losses sustained by the Inhabitants of
this Township by the destruction of their Sheep by Dogs....

ACQUIRING A HOME FOR THE POOR -- 1815

> The set of resolutions submitted
> at a town meeting on April 10,
> 1815, by the committee dealing
> with the acquisition of a home
> for the poor follows.

Source: <u>Records of the Town of Newark, New Jersey</u>, Newark, 1864, pp. 211-212.

The Township Committee hav'g reported that they had
applied to the Legislature of this State and obtained an
Act Entitled "An Act to authorise the Inhabitants of the
Township of Newark in the County of Essex to Build or
Purchase a Poor House."

And also that they had entered into certain Articles
of Agreement in writing on behalf of this Township with
Captain Aa. Johnson, for the purchase of the dwelling
House and farm whereon he lately lived situate in the
Township of Newark, as lately surveyed by Stephen Hayes
Junior, for the sum of Four Thousand Five Hundred Dol-
lars.

Whereupon Resolved that this Township do accept the
Privelidges of the said Act of the Legislature, and do
appoint the said dwelling House and Farm, so as aforesaid agreed by the said Township Committee to be purchased from the said Aaron Johnson, to be the place in
the said Township of Newark to be purchased for a Poor
House according to the terms of the said Act.

Resolved, That the said Township Committee be and
they are hereby empowered to take possession of the said
Dwelling House and farm for the use of the Poor of the
Township, and to receive from the said Aaron Johnson a
Deed for the same--and thereupon the Inhabitants of the
Township of Newark in the County of Essex and their
Successors shall become bound to pay to the said Aaron
Johnson his Executors, Administrators and Assigns the
sum of Four Thousand five hundred Dollars, the consideration money, in manner following to wit--$500 on the first
day of January next with Interest on the whole sum or
Purchase money from the first day of April Instant, and
One thousand Dollars Yearly and Every year thereafter un-
till the whole Purchase money be Paid, with Interest to
be paid Annually on the whole sum remaining unpaid according to the Terms of the said Agreement so made with the
said Aaron Johnson, And that this Township is pledged
and bound to provide the necessary funds to make good the
said Payments.

AN INDEPENDENCE DAY PARADE -- 1821

A list of the floats that appeared
in the Independence Day parade
in 1821 representing the varied
industrial enterprises of the
community follows.

Source: <u>Sentinel of Freedom</u>, July 5, 1821.

AGRICULTURAL REPRESENTATION.

Capt. Moses Baldwin and Daniel Tichenor, two farmers
of distinction, on horseback, with sprigs of wheat in
their hats.
A citizen bearing a stubbing scythe for clearing the
field of briers, etc.
Plough, drawn by four yoke of oxen.
A citizen sowing grain.
Harrow, drawn by two yoke of oxen.
A citizen bearing a cradle, and making the motion of
cutting the waving harvest.
A citizen bearing a rake, significant of raking the
golden sheaves of harvest.
A waggon drawn by one yoke of oxen, loaded with
sheaves, indicating the gathering of the harvest.
A waggon, drawn by two horses on which a stage was
erected; three men were threshing sheaves and another
separating the wheat from the chaff by a fanning mill.
A load of hay drawn by two horses.
Wood's famous patent plough, exhibited on a waggon
and made and sold by E. Meeker & Co.
A large country waggon, with 32 citizens from Orange,
drawn by six horses.

MECHANICAL REPRESENTATION

Moses Harris and Son, merchant tailors: A stage e-
rected on a waggon, drawn by four horses, with a handsome
awning, and a carpet on the floor. Hanging up were seen
a variety of ready-made clothing; also on the shelves--
cloths, cassimeres, vestings, etc.; and one of the firm
ready to receive the orders of customers and several
persons actually at work.
John E. Ruckel, baker; a stage erected on a waggon,
exhibiting stove and fire, and the moulding and baking of
sugar cakes and crackers.
Jacob Alyea's blacksmith's shop, erected on a waggon
drawn by two horses--having forge, bellows, "jobbing of
all kinds." Motto: "July, 1776."
Isaac Nichols' carpenter shop, elevated as before
described exhibiting work bench, chest of tools, saws,

grind stone, etc., and hands at work.

James Nutman and Nathaniel Canfield, masons; their works on a wagon, and a cart attached. In the first were hands at work erecting a fireplace and chimney. In the cart the mason tenders, his brick, mortar, etc. In a sly place we noticed a pitcher and beside it "black betty," probably intended by the labourer to keep up the "spirit" of the day.

Z. Grant & Son, stone cutters; their shop erected on a stage, and all hands busily at work dressing stone.

E. Meeker & Co., potter-bakers; their works erected as above, exhibiting ready made ware, a potter's wheel in operation, etc. Motto: "Success to the Shuttle and Plough."

B. Hall, cotton weaver, with a loom, quill wheel, etc., in operation.

Messrs. Dey, Tice and others, representing the tanners, curriers and morocco dressers. A number of hands were at work, and a variety of leather, calf and morocco skins were exhibited. An elegant flag was erected, emblematical of their profession.

Messrs. Goble and Thomas and Jabez Canfield, boot and shoe manufacturers. Their stages were on two waggons. In front was exhibited a ware-room and persons engaged in packing shoes, writing letters, etc. In the rear a work shop and several hands at work on seats; one of whom made a shoe before the procession entered the church.

Andrew Rankin's hat manufactory, handsomely represented by a sign in front, together with a large kettle set and fire under it; five hands at work sizing hats, one at finishing, one at sewing and one at pulling and cutting muskrat.

Benjamin Cleveland, clock and watchmaker. Messrs. Taylor and Baldwin, jewelers, and Messrs. Downing & Phelps, clock and watchmakers, their establishments being united--near a dozen hands at work at their respective occupations.

David T. Andruss & Co., plane makers; two work benches erected on a stage, and several rabbit, smoothing and fore planers were finished.

John Allen, cabinet maker; three work benches erected, a roping lathe with a supply of tools. The hands were employed in making a bureau bedstead, and roping a sett of table legs.

Hugh M'Dougall, cabinet maker; the stage handsomely ornamented with evergreens; two work benches erected and several hands at work making a cradle, claw work, stands and portable desks.

David Alling's fancy chair establishment, represented by two dozen ready made chairs, and workmen making rush bottom and windsor chairs, together with painting and ornamenting.

D'Coudres & Eagles, tin copper, stove and brass fend-

ers; exhibiting their work benches, smith's forge, copper kettles, brass fenders, stove and tinware.

Aaron Baldwin, gunsmith; exhibiting a number of
guns, fowling pieces, polishing lathe and men at work.

Abner Campbell, tallow chandler; exhibiting moulding
jack, dipping machine, candle wick and candles, all in
complete operation.

Peter Jacobus, saddle and harness maker; exhibiting
a neat shop, with saddles, harnesses, trunks, portman-
teaus, etc.

David Beach's coach making establishments; neatly
constructed on two waggons; exhibiting number of hands
at work on trimming, harness making, woodwork and painting.

Jabez Cook, smith's shop, attached to Mr. Beach's
establishment, having a forge, bellows, etc., erected and
having several hands at work engaged in ironing carriages.

The following six branches were from the Washington
factory (on Mill Brook), each distinguished by appropriate signs.

George' Rohde's coach spring factory; five men at
anvils, filing at springs and putting them together.

Andrew Wilson's silver plating factory, represented
by four men at work.

William Steven's worsted manufactory, represented
by a comber combing wool of various colors, for the spin-
ning machinery, for which machines were very ingeniously
kept in motion by the hind wheels of the waggon. Every
part was kept in complete operation and seven hands were
at work.

William Stevens' coach lace factory, represented
with a loom in full operation, with several other branches of business, and four hands at work.

Thomas Owens' woolen manufactory, represented by
five hands weaving, shearing and dressing cloth; with
flannels, satinets, etc., ready for sale.

Samuel Simpson, stocking weaver, represented by a
loom erected and in full operation; also exhibiting a
number of ready-made articles.

Evans & Owens, chocolate and mustard manufacturers,
handsomely representing their business in a shop, with
a number of hands at work, and their machinery in complete operation.

Peter Tronson, representing the coopering business,
by working at barrels, etc., and exhibiting ready-made
pails and tubs.

Stephen Cooper, pump maker, having a log elevated
on the stage and hands engaged boring and preparing
pumps.

John Paris, hairdresser, with his establishment
neatly rigged on a small waggon, and himself employed in
making a perrywig....

A VISIT FROM LAFAYETTE -- 1824

In September 1824 the Marquis de
Lafayette paid a visit to Newark.

Source: New Jersey Eagle, September 24, 1824.

Yesterday our town had the high satisfaction of
welcoming the illustrious "guest of the nation", Gen. La
Fayette. At nine o'clock in the morning, the General
and family, accompanied by a committee of the New York
corporation, Col. Varick, President, and several members
of the Cincinnati of N. York, together with several other gentlemen of distinction, and a company of dragoons,
was received at Jersey City, from the James Kent, under
a salute from the Artillery by Governor Williamson and
suite. An escort consisting of a division of cavalry
under General Heard, who was an officer of cavalry during the revolution, and who wore his revolutionary uni-
form on this occasion, together with a concourse of citizens was here in waiting to receive, and escort the
party to Newark. On the way hither, the General, who
rode in a barouche drawn by 4 elegant bays, was detained
a few minutes at Bergen, where he was received with a
salute from artillery, and presented with a superb cane,
cut from the apple tree under which La Fayette and Washington once refreshed themselves. The cane was very
elegantly mounted with gold by the Messrs. Bookwells, in
New York, and bore the following inscription - "Shaded
the Hero and his friend Washington in 1779; presented by
the corporation of Bergen in 1824". After this ceremoni-
al, the cavalcade resumed the march and arrived at the
Newark brigade at 12 o'clock, when a national salute was
fired by a detachment of Cadet Artillery, from the
heights on this side of the river. On arriving at the
lines of the town, he was received by the committee of
our citizens, and greeted by the loud and repeated cheers
of the immense throng which had assembled to welcome him.
He was then conducted, amid the constant and unceasing
huzzas of the multitude that thronged the streets through
which he passed, the windows and doors on either side
being also filled with delighted spectators, to the quarters provided for him at the seat of the late Judge Boudinot, into which he passed through lines formed by members of the New Jersey Cincinnati, the Clergy, Civil Authorities, and citizens. During his stay here, the 2nd
Division of N.J. Militia, composed of the Bergen, Essex
and Morris Brigades, (comprising upwards of 2000 troops)
which had been previously formed on the upper common under the command of Major General Doughty, were put in
motion, and marched to the military parade ground....

THE OPENING OF THE MORRIS CANAL -- 1830

An eyewitness account of the December 1830 opening of the Morris
Canal follows.

Source: David Lawrence Pierson, <u>Narrative of Newark (In
New Jersey) From the Days of its Founding, 1666-1916</u>,
Newark, 1917, p. 266.

On December 10, 1830, which was Friday, the incline
plane being completed, we had the pleasure of witnessing
the passage of the first boat through Newark. About 10
o'clock the car descended from the summit of the plane
into the water of the canal behind the hill which
stretches along the west side of the town, till there
was a sufficient depth of water upon the floor of the
car to float the boat upon.

The large and beautiful boat <u>Dover</u>, consigned to
Jonathan Cory, was then towed into the car and secured.
The water was now let in, upon which the large wheel at
the summit and the machinery were set in motion by Major Douglass, the enterprising engineer.

The cable chair was attached to the car and the other end to the machinery, and the car, with the boat
secured within its frame, rose majestically out of the
water with 200 persons aboard.

In six and a half minutes she descended from the
summit to the level of the town and entered her native
element, thus passing a plane 1,040 feet long, overcoming
a descent of 70 feet and advancing forward 770 feet in
an incredibly short space of time.

The boat was then flooded out of the car and drawn
by two horses and as many boys as could get hold of the
tow-line through the town to the lock on the river.

IMPRESSIONS OF A RETURNING NEWARKER -- 1834

> In May 1834 a native-born Newark-
> er, upon returning home after a
> long absence, wrote to a local
> newspaper of his impressions of
> the community.

Source: Frank J. Urquhart, <u>A History of the City of Newark, New Jersey</u>, New York, 1913, vol. I, pp. 568-569.

After an absence of fifteen years, I am again in my native town. On reviewing the place and comparing it to what it was when I left it, I feel emotions both of joy and sorrow arising in my breast. The numerous streets, spires and wharves, proclaim that the population and commerce have spread further and wider, and the hum of business declares that the march of improvement has not yet ceased. Among the most prominent features of improvement which I notice are the canal, a number of churches, splendid rows of brick stores and dwellings, a railroad being constructed, a daily newspaper and a semi-daily communication by land and water with New York; all of which have arisen since I was an inhabitant of Newark.

Yet with all these I do not feel so much gratified as if I had found it in the same condition as I left it. To be sure, there stands the same church and there runs the same river, but yet I cannot realize it as my home. The time was when I could call every inhabitant of the town by name, but now I can walk half a mile in the principal street and every face I meet is a stranger.

Like the great city, it has its haunts of dissipation which have served in a great measure to destroy that innocence and simple beauty which once characterized it.

I have now been here a month, which is long enough to observe the distinguishing traits of character of any town's inhabitants, and although I feel a reluctance to do it, I must say there is a want of public spirit in it. I do not mean a want of enterprise, but there is not enough of care for the general appearance and condition of the town except as far as individual interest is concerned.

Many opportunities offer for beautifying and improving the appearance of the place which are slighted. The condition of the roads is bad, the public houses are not of that class which might be expected and numerous other matters of a public nature are not satisfactorily attended to....

S.F.

THE CITY CHARTER -- 1836

Excerpts from the city charter,
accepted by a public vote on
March 18, 1836, after having
been passed as an act of incorporation by the New Jersey legislature, follow.

Source: Charter of the City of Newark with the Ordinances
and By-Laws Passed by the Common Council, Newark, 1838,
pp. 3-4, 6, 18-20, 30-32.

SEC. 1. Be it enacted by the Council and General
Assembly of this State, and it is hereby enacted by the
authority of the same, That all that district of country
in the county of Essex, contained within the boundary
lines of the township of Newark, as now established by
law, and all the freemen of this State, inhabitants within the limits aforesaid, be and hereby are ordained, con-
stituted and declared to be from time to time and forever
hereafter, one body corporate and politic in fact and in
name, by the name of "The Mayor and Common Council of the
city of Newark," and that by that name, they and their
successors forever shall and may have perpetual succes-
sion, and shall be persons in law capable of suing and
being sued, pleading and being impleaded, answering and
being answered unto, defending and being defended in all
courts and places whatsoever, in all manner of actions,
suits, complaints, matters and causes whatsoever, and that
they and their successors may have a common seal and alter the same at their pleasure, and also by their corporate name aforesaid, shall be in law capable of purchasing, holding and conveying any estate, real or personal,
for the public use of the said corporation, and that the
said, "The Mayor and Common Council of the city of Newark," and their successors shall, by virtue of this act,
become, and be absolutely and completely vested with,
possess and enjoy, all the lands, tenements, hereditaments,
property, rights, causes of action and estate whatsoever,
both in law and equity, in possession, reversion or remainder, which at the time of the passing of this act
are vested in or belong to the inhabitants of the said
township of Newark, in their corporate capacity, as now
incorporated by the name of "The Inhabitants of the township of Newark, in the county of Essex," according to
such estate and interest as the said "The inhabitants of
the township of Newark, in the county of Essex," at the
time of the passage of this act have, or of right ought
to have in the same: Provided, that nothing in this act
contained, shall affect any suit or suits now pending in
the name of "The inhabitants of the township of Newark,

in the county of Essex."

. . .

SEC. 3. And be it enacted, That there be, and forever hereafter there shall be, in and for the said city, one mayor, one recorder, sixteen aldermen, one clerk, two coroners, one treasurer, four assessors, four collectors and twelve constables.

SEC. 4. And be it enacted, That the mayor, recorder, and aldermen of the said city shall constitute and be called the common council of the said city, and the said common council shall be summoned and held at such times and places in the said city, as the mayor, or in his absence or sickness, the recorder of the said city shall appoint, and the mayor or in his absence, the recorder, shall preside at the meetings of the common council, and have a casting vote, and if both be absent, one of the aldermen may be appointed by the members present, pro tempore, and a majority of the whole number of the common council, shall be a quorum to transact business: Provided, that the said mayor, recorder, and aldermen shall not have or exercise any of the powers, duties, or functions of justices of the peace in this State, any thing in the act constituting courts for the trial of small causes, in anywise to the contrary notwithstanding.

. . .

SEC. 20. And be it enacted, That the said city shall beentitled to its just quota of the annual appropriation of the school fund of this state, to be ascertained in the manner in which the quotas of the townships of this state now or hereafter shall be ascertained, which shall be from time to time paid over to the Treasurer of the said city, and be applied under the direction of the school committee, either to the support of the common schools in said city, or to the schooling of poor children of said city, as the Common Council shall by resolution order and direct.

SEC. 21. And be it enacted, That there shall be in and for the said city, eight special police justices, two in each ward of the said city, who shall be appointed by the Council and General Assembly of this state, in joint meeting, and hold their offices for the like term, and be commissioned in the like manner, as justices of the peace in and for the several counties in this state, and be in the like manner amenable to the Council and General Assembly; provided that the said justices shall not by virtue of their said offices, be authorised to hear and try any civil action, except such as may be brought to recover a penalty under the by-laws and ordinances of the said city, in which cases they may severally act as justices of the peace in their civil capacity.

. . .

SEC. 23. And be it enacted, That it shall and may be lawful for the Common Council of the said city, to give and grant unto the Mayor thereof, for the time being, such salary per annum as they shall direct, not exceeding five hundred dollars, payable out of the treasury of the said city, quarter yearly, and the Treasurer and Clerk of said city shall be paid out of said treasury such compensation for their services as the Common Council shall deem reasonable and proper.

. . .

SEC. 38. And be it enacted, That this act shall not go into effect unless the assent of three-fifths of the electors of said townships shall be first ascertained; and for that purpose a poll shall be opened on the eighteenth day of March next, between the hours of ten in the morning, and six in the afternoon, under the direction of the judge and inspectors of election of the respective wards, and at the places where the last annual elections were held; of which time and places the town committee of the township of Newark, shall give at least one week's previous notice in two of the newspapers published in the said township; and the electors entitled to vote at ward meetings, shall express their assent or refusal of this act by depositing their ballots in the box provided for that purpose, in their respective wards; and those electors who are in favor of the said law shall each deposit a ballot containing the word "corporation" written or printed thereon; and those who are opposed shall each deposit a ballot with the words "no corporation" written or printed thereon; and a canvass and return of the votes shall be made by the judges and inspectors of the respective wards in the same manner to the township committee, as is now prescribed by law in regard to the canvass and return of votes for chosen freeholders, surveyors of the highways and school committeemen of the township of Newark; and if three-fifths of those who vote at such elections, at such canvass, are found to be in favor of this act, it shall then, but not otherwise go into effect.

. . .

SEC. 40. And be it enacted, That the legislature may, at any time hereafter, alter, modify or repeal this act.

Passed, Feb. 29, 1836.

THE SEAL OF NEWARK -- 1836

On June 27, 1836, the seal of Newark was adopted, of which a description from the design advisory
committee's report follows.

Source: Frank J. Urquhart, A History of the City of Newark, New Jersey, New York, 1913, vol. II, pp. 617-618.

On the right is a female figure seated; her right
hand resting upon the hilt of a sword, her left suspending a scales, in equal balance. On the left is a
female figure in a standing posture sustaining with her
right hand the standard and cap of liberty, and her left
arm resting on a bundle of rods, holding the olive
branch. Between these figures is a shield, on which
three ploughs are represented; above is the dexter arm
suspending a hammer. Encircling the whole are the letters and figures following, "Newark City Seal, Incorporated, 1836."

THE NEW CITY HALL AND COURT HOUSE BUILDING -- 1836

        In August 1836 the cornerstone of
        the city hall and court house
        building was laid.

Source: <u>Newark Daily Advertiser</u>, August 25, 1836.

        The ceremonies of laying the corner stone of this
edifice took place yesterday. The Municipal authorities
of the City, and Chosen Freeholders of the County, with
the Chief Justice and other judicial officers of the
State and County, the Chief Architect, and his corps of
laborers, &c., &c., formed a procession at the Common
Council chamber at 3 o'clock, and proceeded to the site
under the direction of Sheriff Robinson.
        After the Sheriff reached the place, the title of
the ground was presented to his Honor the Mayor of the
City, Wm. H. Halsey, Esq., by the donors, and by him
transferred to the Freeholders of the County. Statements
were then made by Mr. J. W. Condit and Dr. Wm. Pierson,
of the proceedings of the County and City in relation to
the joint erection of the building--with an exhibition
of the plans, and the contract made with the architect.
Previous to the laying of the corner stone, the Hon.
Stephen D. Day, director of the Board of Freeholders,
made an address. . . . Mr. Halsey then proceeded with
some highly interesting reminiscences of the history of
the Court House of Essex. . . . After also briefly re-
capitulating the terms of union between City and County,
the speaker remarked: "that by this union the interest of
the county has become more particularly identified with
the interest of the City. A natural union, like that of
a parent with a child, united to build in connection, a
dwelling for the mutual accommodation--an union, the effect of which will be economy, a saving to both parties--
an union the effect of which will be a magnificent building, creditable to the State, the County, and the City--
central in its situation, convenient in its construction,
and of materials durable as time."

SUPPLYING THE FIRST FIRE HYDRANTS WITH WATER
1846

            In May 1846 the first fire hy-
            drants were supplied with water.

Source: <u>Newark Daily Advertiser</u>, May 15, 1846.

        The experiments made by the Fire Department yester-
day to test the capacity of the Hydrants recently put
up by the city authorities for the supply of water for
extinguishing fires proved entirely satisfactory, as we
learn from the Mayor /Beach Vanderpool7, at whose request
they were made. Various trials were made with Hydrants
in both Broad and Market streets. . . . The sufficiency
and value of this admirable arrangement for the supply of
water may therefore be considered as placed beyond a
peradventure--which is a subject for general congratulation.

A RECOMMENDATION FOR ESTABLISHING
THE POLICE DEPARTMENT -- 1857

In his annual mesage on January 6,
1857, Mayor Moses Bigelow made a
recommendation that led to the establishment of a modern-type police department.

Source: Joseph Fulford Folsom, The Municipalities of
Essex County, New Jersey, 1664-1924, New York, 1925,
vol. I, p. 168.

The present organization of the police and of
Watch department, I think very defective. The peace and
tranquility of the city and the security and protection
of the property of citizens require an active and ener-
getic performance of the duties of each department. The
service rendered under the present organization is alto-
gether inadequate to the expense incurred. I would recommend that it be made a subject of your inquiry whether
it would not be more economical and whether the energy
and efficiency of each would not be promoted by re-organi-
zing the police and watch departments and putting them
under one head.

PROTESTING MILITARY CONSCRIPTION -- 1863

> In July 1863 mobs protested the
> conscription of men to fight in
> the Civil War for the Union.

Source: <u>Newark Daily Advertiser</u>, July 14, 1863.

Our city was last evening the scene of a riotous
demonstration which, though attended with comparatively
trifling results, was still sufficient to create considerable excitement and alarm. On some accounts it
may be regarded fortunate, inasmuch as it tended to
forewarn our authorities in a manner that will cause
them to be forearmed against any more serious consequences in the future.

It apparently arose without any premeditation or
concert of action among a large group of people, who
had casually assembled to hear and discuss the news of
the New-York riots, though it is alleged that it was in-
stigated by parties from New York who came up in one of
the evening trains, but this is improbable, for the men
appeared to have no leaders, nor any settled purpose.

Upon the reception of the news of the riot in New-
York yesterday, crowds assembled about the bulletin
boards, and shortly after nightfall a large concourse
had gathered and was eagerly engaged in discussing the
affair. Many sensation reports were in circulation, and
only added fuel to the already kindled flame. The dis-
cussions became warmer and warmer, and at last the crowd
gave cheers for the New-York conscripts, State rights,
VALLANDIGHAM, Govs. SEYMOUR and PARKER, Gen. RUNYON,
Mayor /MOSES/ BIGELOW and others, and groans for LINCOLN,
GREELEY, Provost-Marshal MILLER, his guard, &c. One
elderly gentleman, named STAINSBROUGH, was assailed and
struck in the face, the blow drawing blood, his hat was
torn from his head, and he was compelled to seek refuge
in a neighborhood store.

The crowd having thus commenced their attack, moved
across Broad-street to the <u>Mercury</u> office, and commenced
a series of groans for everything connected with the Administration, intermingled with cheers for their favor-
ites. Cries were made of "Down with the wheel," "We won't
be drafted," "The wheel's broken," "Where are your $300?"
&c., &c. Threats were made to sack and burn the building, but at that time nothing was done beyond threats.
Capt. S. C. FORDHAM, late of the Twenty-sixth regiment,
was assailed, but escaped uninjured.

At about 10 o'clock a young man arose upon the
stoop, and indulged in a series of inflammatory remarks
about the wrongs of VALLADIGHAM, the abolitionism of
THADDEUS STEVENS, the alledged imparyiality and injustice

of the Conscription, its hazards to the poor man, &c.,
had closed by demanding that, as the Journal office had
been compelled to show a flag some eighteen months since,
the same should now be done by the Mercury. This remark
was met with cheers and cries of "Show the flag," "We'll
give you five minutes," &c. There being no one in the
office at this time, the demand was not then complied
with, but a small flag was subsequently raised.

To a cry of "Down with the door" a rush was made,
and in a moment or two the door at the foot of the stairs
was torn to pieces and scattered about the streets. The
cry of "Stones" was then made, and the crowd, supplying
themselves with these missiles from materials for the
new building of the City Bank, commenced an assault
on the building, and in a short time demolished several
windows.

A number of policemen, some ten or fifteen in number,
had by this time collected, but, owing to their mispro-
portion to the crowd, they could do nothing effective.
There was, however, one exception, Sergt. HENRY HAURY,
who, though of small stature, boldly placed himself in
the door, and kept the crowd back so far as possible. He
also went into the building, found a flag and raised it,
amid cheers from the mob.

Their demands having been complied with, after a few
more volleys of stones, the mob proceeded to the resi-
dence of Provost-Marshal MILLER, in Fulton-street, shout-
ing and yelling the entire distance. Some friends of Mr.
MILLER, anticipating their arrival, had notified him,
and the family was removed to a place of safety, while a
few personal friends of Mr. MILLER remained to protect
him. For some time they were in doubt as to the house
(Mr. MILLER having recently moved,) but by the aid of
a light and examining the various door plates the location was at last found.

The mob then moved to the front, and amid shouts of
"Miller," "Hang him," &c., began to hurl stones against
the doors and windows. The darkness of the night, the
falling rain and some dense shade-trees interfered with
their aim, and the damage was comparatively trifling....

MOURNING PRESIDENT LINCOLN'S DEATH -- 1865

> In April 1865 the residents
> mourned the death of Presi-
> dent Abraham Lincoln.

Source: <u>Newark Daily Advertiser</u>, April 20, 1865.

If any doubt had before existed as to the profound
grief of the people over the death of ABRAHAM LINCOLN,
the obsequies of yesterday must have entirely dissipated
it. The whole city was literally in mourning. A deep
solemnity seemed to pervade the very atmosphere.--Busi-
ness was everywhere suspended, and an almost Sabbath
stillness rested upon the crowded streets. Men seemed
to demean themselves, as if in the death of the lamented
Chief Magistrate, they had sustained a personal loss; as
if being one of themselves, representing in his whole
career their needs, their convictions and aspirations,
his removal touched them in the tenderest relations of
kinship and affection.--No city in the Union has ever
paid to any man, living or dead, a more tearful, generous,
whole-souled tribute of admiration and love than Newark
yesterday paid to the great and good ruler whose hand
shall never again hold up the standard of the people or
lead them in the struggle for unity and peace.
The outward semblances of mourning were universal,
and only fell short of the actual feeling of sorrow
which pervaded all hearts.--Throughout the whole line of
Broad street, almost every building was conspicuous in
black and white testimonials of grief--many of the designs being novel and tasteful, and in a number of cases
remarkably artistic--and there seemed, indeed, to exist
an emulation among the citizens in doing honor to the
memory of the lamented dead.
It would be a difficult and unnecessary task to de-
scribe minutely the appearance of each building where the
arrangement of funeral draperies displayed unusual taste,
but some more prominent features of this sombre exhibition may be mentioned. The front of the Post Office was
heavily and elegantly upholstered in black and white,
and bore this inscription, short but comprehensive--"THE
NATION MOURNS." The building occupied by the Provost
Marshal was also very effectively decorated with the sad
habiliments of mourning, each window being draped with
black and white and one containing the initial L., surrounded with a wreath of evergreen. The Hospital was
tastefully draped both inside and out with black and
white.--Union shields, with rosettes of mourning, each
containing the portrait of Abraham Lincoln, beneath which
inscribed the sentence "THE NATION MOURNS ITS LOSS." In
another position over the portraits of Washington and

Lincoln was the inscription, "The Fathers of our Country have met." Many private residences were elegantly and appropriately draped and bore suitable inscriptions. O-ver the portico of one on the line of march, appeared in white letters on a field of black the simple word "Alas!" and in this natural and expressive interjection of grief seemed to be concentrated all the sorrow and woe of the hour. In a number of windows were exhibited likenesses of the thoughtful and melancholy countenance of him the nation mourns, surrounded with crape and accompanied by suitable mottoes. In many places were to be seen amid the mourning devices sentences expressive of the general feeling. In front of one store in Broad street the out-line of a monument was presented bearing a wreath and the name of "Lincoln;" beneath it the couplet--"Whether by the assassins hand or in the battle van, The fittest place for man to die is where he dies for man." In another place on a mortuary urn was inscribed the motto "Dulco et Decorum est pro patria mori." In still another the sen-tence "Our leader has fallen, but duty still is ours," and in a position in Market street these words of com-fort--"God is our refuge and strength, a very present help in trouble."

But not only in the principal avenues through which the mournful procession moved, and at the stores and residences of the wealthy, were to be seen these evi-dences of the public grief, but in the smaller stores, byways and alleys far from the route of march, the hum-blest tenements were darkened with the drapery of mourning, which hung in the windows, or a little piece of black muslin draped from the abodes of poverty gave evidence of the strong hold President Lincoln possessed upon the affections of the people of all classes. Of a truth it seemed as if on this day every dwelling was under the shadow of affliction, and as if from every household was to be carried forth the beloved head, with tears and lamentations.

THE CHURCHES--THE PROCESSION

Upon the tolling of the bells the people at 12 o'-clock assembled in the various churches in accordance with the Governor's proclamation, where religious ser-vices suitable to the solemn occasion took place and ap-propriate addresses were made. Shortly after two o'clock, with rare and commendable promptness, the funeral pro-cession started on its march from the neighborhood of the Military Park following the route already published....

CELEBRATING THE TWO HUNDREDTH ANNIVERSARY
OF NEWARK'S FOUNDING -- 1866

The celebration in May of the two
hundredth anniversary of the founding of Newark took place with a
variety of activities.

Source: Newark Daily Advertiser, May 18, 1866.

The occasion of the celebration of the Bi-Centennial
Anniversary of the Settlement of Newark will be long remembered. Much of the pomp and parade with which it was
intended to honor the day was prevented by the gloomy
rain which ushered in the morning and continued in inter-
vals during the day, yet so deep was the interest felt by
all classes of citizens that even those unfavorable circumstances could not control them and the display was
exceedingly creditable to the public spirit of the city.
We published yesterday the action taken at the meeting
of the New Jersey Historical Society, held in the morning. It remains to put on record the trasactions of the
afternoon and evening.

EXERCISES IN THE CHURCH

The doors of the old First Presbyterian Church were
thrown open at the appointed hour, and that ancient and
historic edifice was soon filled with an audience composed of representatives of all classes in our community
and of every age: the white haired patriarchs, linking
the present with the commemorated past, and the children
destined to carry the reminiscences of this anniversary
occasion far into the new century. A platform had been
erected around the pulpit and this was occupied by Governor Marcus L. Ward and his staff, consisting of the following: Gens. N. N. Halsted, W. H. Penrose, and E. A.
Carman; Cols. R. S. Swords and J. W. Woodruff, and Dr.
A. N. Dougherty; Mayor Thomas B. Peddie; the orator,
officers of the New Jersey Historical Society, clergy of
the city, and representatives from other societies as
follows: New York Historical Society--Hon. George Ban-
croft, Hon. John R. Brodhead, Judge Charles P. Kirkland;
Pennsylvania Historical Society--Horatio G. Jones, Charles
E. McCallister, J. S. African; American Antiquarian So-
ciety--Nathaniel Paine, of Worcester, Massachusetts; The
Historical and Genealogical Societies of Massachusetts--
J. H. Shepperd; Connecticut Historical Society--Erastus
Smith.

On one side of the pulpit a large colored copy of
the map of "OUR TOWNE ON PASAYAK RIVER," as originally
laid out in 1866, was displayed, and on the other the
. . . names of the first settlers. . . .

A VOTE FOR RUNNING STREETCARS ON SUNDAYS -- 1869

> In June 1869 the residents voted
> to repeal the city ordinance pro-
> hibiting the running of horse-
> drawn streetcars on Sundays.

Source: <u>Newark Daily Advertiser</u>, June 2, 1869.

The special election yesterday for a direct expression of opinion of the people on the subject of running the horse cars on Sunday, resulted in a majority of
nearly three thousand in favor of the measure. In the
13th ward the vote was nearly unanimous--less than 100
being cast against it, while over 1200 voted in favor;
in the 6th ward there was also a large majority, the
vote being 673 for, to 137 against. In the 11th ward
the vote was very close, the influence of Rev. Father
Dalton of St. Joseph's church having been thrown against
the movement.
The First and Third and Ninth wards gave small ma-
jorities against the running, while all the other wards
voted for it. The vote was quite small, less than two
thirds of the vote usually cast at the elections, having
been polled yesterday. In the inner wards many of the
best citizens and largest property owners failed to vote.
The following is the vote in detail, together with
the total vote cast at the general election last fall:

Wards	For	Against.	Maj. For	Maj. Against.	Total 1869.	Total 1868.
1....	308	424		116	732	1257
2....	536	368	168		904	1480
3....	388	537		149	925	1282
4....	503	273	230		776	1373
5....	582	284	298		886	1533
6....	673	137	536		810	1364
7....	589	393	196		982	1762
8....	497	232	175		639	1060
9....	296	394		92	690	1082
10...	460	295	165		755	1363
11...	128	115	13		243	472
12...	397	16	381		413	600
13...	1219	95	1124		1314	1631
	6486	3563	3286	363	10049	16262

Total majority in favor of running. 2923.
The subject will come before the Common Council on
Friday evening when the ordinance prohibiting the Sunday
travel, will probably be repealed and the privilege thus
thrown open to the managers of the companies to avail
themselves of if they chose....

THE THIRD ANNUAL NEWARK INDUSTRIAL
EXHIBITION -- 1874

The third annual Newark Industrial
Exhibition, in which goods produced in the city were on display,
was held in October 1874.

Source: <u>New York Times</u>, October 24, 1874.

The third annual Industrial Exposition of Newark,
N. J., is now thoroughly under way at the Rink, on Washington street in that city. The exhibition is confined
exclusively to goods manufactured in Newark, except in
the matter of curiosities and antiquities. Newark has
long been celebrated for the manufacture of carriages,
and in this department is probably not excelled by any
city in the United States or in the world. This year
the stock exhibited will be of a finer quality than that
of any previous exposition, and will comprise landaus,
close carriages, barouches, extension top phaetons, English pony phaetons, and rockaways. Some of these are
very elegant, and are valued as high as $1,800. In this
connection, some choice sleighs and substantial express
wagons are well worthy of examination. Newark is also
the great manufacturing depot for trunks and leatherbags.
A very large proportion of New-York wholesale trunk establishments have their factories here, and the samples
and styles exhibited at the Rink are as near perfection
as possible. A trained baggage-smasher would become de-
jected at his incompetency to destroy some of them. The
display of boots and shoes is such that were they la-
beled as the manufacture of a Parisian Crispin, no one
would raise a question. Of fur goods, for the manufacture of which Newark has long enjoyed a high reputation,
some excellent specimens were shown. The exhibition of
silver ware and silver-plated ware is superior in style
and pattern, and fully deserving the admiration which it
everywhere elicits.
In horse equipments and carriage appurtenances the
exhibition is remarkably complete. Saddles of every variety, bridles, harness, carriage-lamps, &c., with gold
and silver platings, fill a large space in the exposition. Mechanics' tools of every description are also exhibited, as well as saws, files, weights, scales, measures, the most intricate locks, finely plated faucets,
spoons, &c., &c.
There is an extensive show of Newark cutlery, equal
in many respects to the finest Sheffield goods. The
suites of parlor and chamber furniture exhibited by several prominent manufacturers are unique in design, and
finished with the most careful regard to detail. Con-

spicuous in the display of hard wood mantels are several
admirable patterns, adorned with carved female busts,
dog's heads, birds, &c. As in a measure belonging to
fine house furniture, reference should be made to a number of very complicated stair newels, beautiful in design and rich in artistic carvings and adornments. One
is remarkable for having a regular clock worked in its
crown or head piece. Several varieties of pianos and
sewing-machines are also exhibited.

Baxter's steam engine, invented and constructed by
a citizen of Newark, is a remarkably compact arrangement
for the application of steam power. The specimens exhibited are of two-horse power and upward.

Newark fully indorses the sentiment, "that there
is nothing like leather," and judging from the extraor-
dinary display of this tough material, she lives up to
her creed. In this line of goods are some mammoth specimens of finished hides, one of which is said to measure 98 square feet. The display of dye-stuffs, chemi-
cals, acids, crystals, &c., is likewise very extensive.

Among other objects of interest is a large collection of ancient coins, belonging to several citizens of
Newark. In the Roman department are some which bear
"images and superscriptions" from Ptolemy I., B. C. 323,
to Honorius, A. D. 423. Coins are also exhibited of
nearly all the countries of Europe, as well as Continental and Confederate money. A quantity of cigars, tastefully arranged in a lofty glass case some twelve or fourteen feet high, have a very unique appearance. There is
a huge display of ornamental cut-glass for drawing-room
and vestibule doors; some of the designs of which are
new and original. The same may be said of several elab-
orate specimens of iron-railing, highly ornamented and
gilded.

Besides the ordinary medicated vapor baths, several
portable baths are exhibited. These last are intended
for use in traveling.

Much merit is evinced in the fancy confectionery on
exhibition. Of the pieces presented, two, Gen. Kearney's
charge in the military action which cost him his life,
and an allegorical temple of true architectural propor-
tions, ornamented with figures and emblems, are particularly deserving of mention. "A fountain in metal" is a
fine work of art. A bull-frog is perched upon a stone,
and his mouth, when the fountain is in operation, forms
the jet d'eau. Two dogs, in the most natural attitudes,
are represented as capering about the unwonted spectacle.
The display of fine wax-work is extensive. The same may
be said of the exhibition of children's carriages and
wagons. Plows, specimens of granite work, a steam fire-
engine, a miniature engine of dainty workmanship, pearl
manufactured goods, brushes, elis, tin ware, highly-col-
ored woolen mats and rugs are prominently exhibited. . . .

A PROFILE OF NEWARK -- 1876

An excerpt of a profile of Newark
published in October 1876 by Martha J. Lamb follows.

Source: Martha J. Lamb, "Newark," Harper's New Monthly
Magazine, LIII, October 1876, p. 673.

It /Broad Street/is one of the widest and finest avenues
on this continent. It is not only the great business,
but the social centre of a city which spreads over an
area of eighteen or more square miles. And it was created in the beginning. Its bank, insurance, and mercan-
tile blocks are substantial, and in many instances elegant. Its churches illustrate the ornate architecture
of the period. The northern and southern portions are
deeply shaded with magnificent trees. Here, in digni-
fied mansions, reside the families enriched by the industry of the busy town. The southern portion of the
street is now, more strictly speaking, Newark's West End.
In former years the aristocracy clustered about the en-
chanting parks to the north. The stately homes of such
ancient and important families as the Frelinghuysens, the
Hornblowers, the Wrights, the Wards, the Days, the Hal-
seys, the Van Antwerps, the Nicolls, and many others
still ornament this part of Broad Street.
     About midway Broad is crossed at right angles by
Market, another exceptionally wide street, also an an-
cestral legacy. The neighborhood of the intersection is
the great pivot of the city's trade and commerce, which
extends to every quarter of the civilized globe. Market
Street rises, in district-school parlance, in the court-
house, on the western hill-side, and empties into the
railroad depot, to the east. From the top of the court-
house you look down upon a perfectly straight street,
filled with horse-cars and vehicles of every sort and description, while the sidewalks are half hidden from view
by boxes and bales and moving throngs of people. The
sight on a week-day morning, about seven o'clock, is
something to be remembered; an army of men, women, and
children, the latter of all ages, fill both street and
sidewalks as they proceed to their various employments.
There never was a more useful thoroughfare than Market
Street. It is none too broad. And it is exactly where
it should be. It drains that portion of the city which
sits upon a hill. And a very large portion of the city
seems to sit on the hill, or upon the billows of hills
and picturesque elevations which overlook the sea of
brick and foliage upon the plains below. To the right
and left of you runs High Street, parallel with Broad.
It is very properly named, although the brow of the

heights is not yet reached. It is lined with handsome
private residences, planted at easy distances from each
other, amidst leafy and flowery surroundings, and has
the smooth pavement which renders it a favorite drive.
The streets which connect it with Broad Street are a
little too steep for comfort, but by a gradual descent
to the south, where elegant mansions dot the soil as far
as the eye can reach, and a mild detour, you will find
yourself upon the common level. To the west, north, and
northwest of the court-house the better class of dwellings prevail, the more noticeable the farther you go.
Tasteful villas are scattered here and there, but their
grounds have been clipped off at the edges by the scis-
sors of industry, and they are closely pushed by rows of
ambitious cottages, school-houses, and great unsightly
mills. To the southwest the Germans have built a city
of their own,....

To return to Broad Street. It is in itself a great
historical monument. It was along its line that the
first settlers built their houses. As soon as they had
obtained a double title to the land, they laid out the
town. Some few demurred because so much of the earth's
surface was turned into roads, but the shrewd discern-
ment of the leading minds would not abate an inch, hence
the broad, beautiful main streets and extensive public
squares which are the present glory of Newark. Military
Park was designed as a military parade ground, and was
called the Lower Green; Washington Square was for a mar-
ket-place, and was known as the Upper Green. Each man
contributed equally to the cost of the property, and then
drew by lot six acres for a homestead. Before the drawing the gallant Robert Treat was courteously given the
choice of a home lot of eight acres. He fixed upon the
southeast corner of Broad and Market streets, where his
descendants resided until the commencement of the present
century. A number of "tradesmen's lots" were set apart
to be given to the first of any trade who should settle
permanently in the place. Each man was bound by an a-
greement to bear an equal share in all public burdens,
such as clearing, ditching the meadows, fencing, killing
wolves, etc., and the time to perform such service was
regulated with the precision of a military manoeuvre.

ANARCHISTS IN A LABOR DAY PARADE -- 1893

> During a Labor Day parade in Sep-
> tember 1893 demonstrating members
> of an anarchist organization were
> routed by the police.

Source: <u>New York Times</u>, September 5, 1893.

A bold attempt to flaunt the red flag as an adjunct
to today's Labor Day demonstration in this city was frus-
trated by the action of Capt. Glori and the Fourth Precinct police.

The trick resorted to by the long-haired men who recently made such a fizzle of the "hunger parade" was worthy of a better cause.

The central body of the Newark Anarchists has its
headquarters in Pollock Hall, 43 Prince Street. In the
same building Laborers' Protective Union No. 2 and the
Brewers' Union hold their business meetings. The members
are nearly all Germans, and had to hold picnics of their
own to-day independent of the general picnic.

They extended an invitation to the Anarchists to
participate with them, not because they are in sympathy
with their teachings, but because of occupying the same
hall.

The unions went out in the general parade and marched
to the corner of South Orange Avenue and Jones Street,
where they left the general parade and started over Jones
Street to Ester's and Oertel's Park, while their compan-
ions went on to Schuetzen Park.

They had asked for no permit for this parade, but
the wily Anarchists who joined them at this point had
procured one in the name of the unions.

The permit was granted on Aug. 24, and on Sunday
Capt. Charles Glori learned that there was great jubila-
tion in Anarchistic circles over the manner in which the
police had been tricked, and also that they intended to
display the red flag. He notified Superintendent Brown,
and the latter wrote to Unant, who procured the permit,
calling his attention to the manner in which the permit
had been granted and threatening arrest if anything but
the Stars and Stripes appeared in line. Unant made no
reply.

When the laborers and brewers turned into Jones
Street they were met by about sixty Anarchists.

The police had been on the lookout, and Capt. Cor-
bett, who commanded the mounted police in the big parade,
remarked something which looked suspiciously like a red
flag carefully guarded by a quartet in the centre of the
group. He galloped through Hayes Street and notified
Capt. Glori, who met the paraders just as they turned in-

to Fifteenth Avenue. He allowed the unions to pass, and
then with a squad of men blocked the progress of the Anarchists.

One of the Anarchists carried a long pole bearing a
placard inscribed:

"The red flag cannot be carried in Newark."

Directly behind him in a hollow square came four men
holding taut by the corners a large red silk flag.

Despite their obstinate resistance and fighting every inch of the way Capt. Glori broke through the line
and tore the flag from their grasp. All but one relin-
quished their hold, and after this one was knocked down
by a well-directed blow, the Captain ordered the crowd
to disperse and started for the precinct with his tro-
phy.

Four of the Anarchists, Andrew Moeller, William
Stvettgen, Carl Kappe, and Abraham Cigierich followed the
Captain, and when they found him alone fell upon him and
recaptured their flag. They ran, but were caught after a
short chase, and were taken, with the flag, to the police
station and locked up.

Then the mounted men charged on the mob and put them
to flight without any further trouble.

TYPHOID FEVER OUTBREAK ATTRIBUTED TO
STREET PAVING ·-- 1896

> In April 1896 city health offi-
> cials attributed the many out-
> breaks of typhoid fever to the
> use of sand from the Passaic
> River in paving the streets.

Source: <u>New York Times</u>, April 27, 1896.

The city health authorities have been puzzling their
brains for some time to find the cause of numerous outbreaks of typhoid fever. Finally Dr. H. C. H. Herold,
President of the Board of Health, hit upon the cause.
The discovery is causing much talk in medical circles.
His discovery is that the outbreaks are due to street
paving.

Dr. Herold first noticed that the streets being
paved or repaired were those in which the disease started.
The sand used in paving is taken from the bed of the
Passaic River. Some of it subjected to a bacteriological
examination showed the presence of bacillus resembling
typhoid. The examination was conducted by Dr. Connolly
at the suggestion of Dr. Herold. City Chemist Baldwin
made an analysis of some of the sand and found an odor of
sewage, and also free and albuminoid ammonia. Two samples of cultures were sent to the New-York Board of Health
and the results of the operations there confirmed the
finding of the local experts.

Medical men express great surprise that sand from
the Passaic River should have been used in the work when
it was commonly known that the water and the river bed
are reeking with filth and disease germs. The Health Department did not know the source of the sand supply for
a long time, and supposed it was dug from some hillside.
The specifications call for "sharp" sand, and this can
be obtained only from places where there is a constant
movement of sand.

It is alleged that not only is sand from the river
used in city work, but that sand taken from the bottoms
of manholes in the sewers is used to repair crosswalks.
This sand is even worse than river sand. Until recently
all the sand used in street paving has been obtained from
the vicinity of Metuchen. It is, of course, cheaper to
dredge sand from the river bed, as it saves hauling.

THE CATALOGUE OF THE NEWARK ACADEMY -- 1900

>   Excerpts from the 1900 catalogue
>   of the Newark Academy, a boys
>   preparatory school, follow.

Source: <u>Catalogue of the Newark Academy</u>, Newark, 1900,
pp. 1-2, 10.

The object of this circular is to give to the pa-
trons of the Academy and others who may be interested a
more detailed statement in regard to certain matters
than can be given in the annual catalogue.

The total enrolment of pupils during the past year
has been 263, a slight increase over that of the preceding year.

In the eleven years preceding this the Academy has
sent out 223 graduates; 154 have entered college. Of
this number Princeton has taken 83, Yale 26, Columbia
12, Rutgers 8, Stevens 6, Massachusetts Institute of
Technology 3, Lafayette 3, Cornell 2, Amherst 2, Wesleyan 2, New York University 2, Brown 2, Williams 1, Le-
high 1, and University of California 1. A number have
also entered various professional schools.

The graduating class this year numbers 24, 10 in the
Classical course, 7 in the Scientific, and 7 in the Latin Scientific. In addition to these six boys have completed special courses of study, but have not fulfilled
the requirements necessary to secure diplomas. Nearly
all of these six are boys from other schools who have
come to the Academy for a last year of work before entering college or going into business.

Of the entire number 24 will enter college, 13 going
to Princeton, 4 to Stevens, 3 to Columbia, and 1 each to
Harvard, Rutgers, Cornell and Wesleyan.

                    . . .

This institution was organized in 1792, incorporated
in 1795, and rechartered in 1855. It is a stock company,
with a dividend. All profits, therefore, are applied to
the improvement of the school. It is controlled by a
Board of Trustees, elected by the stockholders.

It affords a complete and thorough course of study,
fitting for any college or scientific school, or for
business life. There are three courses: the Classical,
the Scientific and the Latin Scientific, each extending
through five years. Pupils finishing satisfactorily either of these courses are entitled to the diploma of the
Academy. Variations from the regular courses are arranged to meet the requirements of different colleges,
and in the later years of the Scientific and Latin Scientific courses considerable choice is given to the individual student. Special courses may be arranged....

A REPORT OF THE NEWARK BOARD OF TRADE -- 1903

> The report of the Committee on
> Public Health of the Newark
> Board of Trade (the forerunner
> of the Chamber of Commerce of
> the City of Newark) for 1903
> follows.

Source: <u>Year Book of the Board of Trade</u>, Newark, 1903,
pp. 54-55.

GENTLEMEN:--Your Health Committee, being the first
of its kind, in the history of the Newark Board of Trade,
have felt at a loss as to the extent or character of investigation required.

But we have had several sub-committees at work, and
desire to report to you on their findings.

The Committee on Garbage Disposal has investigated
the matter and have reported that the separation of the
garbage and the use of the so-called "Arnold-Edgerton"
system, for the reduction of the garbage proper, has now
been conceded by the great majority of authorities, to be
one of the best systems, and we congratulate the proper
authorities of our city for having instituted this much
needed reform.

The Committee on Vaccination and Smallpox have reported in favor of a compulsory vaccination law, and
would respectfully refer to the disappearance of the disease even in winter, after those not immune, have been
vaccinated as has been the case in this as well as other
cities.

From correspondence had, with other cities, concerning the handling of an outbreak of small pox in large
cities, your committee believes that time, money and
life, will be saved by the strict quarantining of all
subjects and contaminated houses and persons, at the outbreak of an epidemic, a procedure, evidently not practi-
cable, later on, when there are many houses and persons
affected.

Another subject considered, was the disinfection of
public library and school books, members of your committee, have frequently seen school and library books on
the beds and in the rooms of scarlet fever, diphtheria
and smallpox patients. It is believed that some action
should be taken in this matter.

Your committee have also given some attention to
the condition of the streets, which have now for some
four months been almost entirely neglected. The increased
prevalence of disease under such conditions is well
known. Careful statistics taken in New York, have shown
a well marked ratio between the conditions of the streets

and disease among the people exposed to these conditions.
    Many of the trolley cars of Newark are positively
filthy, and very few are properly lighted and ventilated.
Your Committee has also considered the condition of the
public bath houses and while we feel that each new bath
house shows some improvement upon the older ones in mi-
nor respects, we would, however strongly recommend the
doing away with the common pool bath and the substitution therefor, the individual shower bath, upon the
ground of cleanliness and the entire freedom from conta-
gion.
    Your Committee desires to distinctly call your at-
tention to the very great danger to public health, arising from the existence, in the most thickly populated
portion of the city, of an immense open sewer, called
"The Morris Canal." It is bad now, but in spring and
summer, it is very much worse. Any private citizen,
who pays taxes, maintaining one-hundredth part as great
a nuisance, would be sued by the health authorities at
once.
    All of which is respectfully submitted, for the
Committee on Public Health.

DUTIES OF THE MAYOR -- 1904

The official duties of the mayor
in 1904 follow.

Source: Manual of the Common Council, Newark, N. J.,
Newark, 1904, p. 165.

He may give permission to examine public records.

He has power to revoke general licenses, to sign
temporary loan bonds, to sign record of engrossed ordinances, to approve bills allowed by Council, to approve
all resolutions passed by Council, to sign all warrants.

To grant the following permits: For street stands
during the holidays and at 4th of July; to allow banners
across public streets; for fireworks exhibitions.

To appoint the following officers subject to approval by the Council: Tax Commissioners, Police Commissioners, Fire Commissioners, Comptroller, Auditor, Members of
the Board of Health.

To appoint the following officers not subject to
confirmation by Council: City Counsel, City Attorney,
Assistant City Attorney, Excise Commissioners, Trustees
of Free Public Library, Assessment Commissioners, Police
Justices, Private Secretary, Clerk in Executive Department.

Member ex-officio of the following commissions:
Sinking Fund, Public Library, Newark City Home, Finance
Committee.

THE ANNUAL MESSAGE OF MAYOR HAUSSLING -- 1907

Excerpts from the annual message
of Mayor Jacob Haussling, delivered in January 1907, follow.

Source: The First Message of Jacob Haussling, Mayor,
Presented to the Common Council of the City of Newark,
New Jersey, January Third, Nineteen Hundred and Seven,
Newark, 1907, pp. 5-9, 14-15.

CONGESTION OF TRAFFIC

The congestion of vehicular traffic at the intersection of the two chief arteries of travel--Broad and
Market streets--is daily becoming a more serious problem. Not alone does the situation involve costly incon-
venience and delay to the business interests of the city,
but the lives and limbs of citizens are constantly im-
periled. Various remedies are proposed, such as the di-
version of certain kinds of vehicles, the abolition of
certain switches or curved rails, and the changing of
street railway lines, for each of which something can be
said.

But all of these might truthfully be termed mere
expedients of half measures, which if adopted would afford merely temporary relief. The time has come in my o-
pinion for Newark, through its public bodies, to give
careful consideration to the subject of a subway for the
trolley cars which add so greatly to the congestion at
the point indicated. In no other way, I believe, can
permanent relief be secured.

The conditions in this city in this respect resemble
in many ways those prevailing in the city of Boston.
There as here a vast number of trolley car lines, drain-
ing an extensive and densely populated territory, converge
at one point in the centre of the city. Until the Boston
subway was completed the congestion was even more serious
than in Newark. The removal of the trolley car lines
from the surface of the street has wrought such a won-
derful change as almost to seem miraculous.

I earnestly recommend that the Common Council and
the Board of Street and Water Commissioners enter upon a
careful study of this suggestion, both from the financial
and the engineering points of view. It may not be amiss
to remark that such property as may be required by the
city in the progress of such an undertaking can never a-
gain be acquired as cheaply as at the present time. Without having been able to examine sufficiently into the subject to be certain on this point, I believe that a subway
could be built by the city and leased on such terms as
would pay all interest and sinking fund charges, thus

leaving no expense of the work to be borne by the tax-payers.

While not acquainted with the views of the officials charged with the management of the trolley lines, I apprehend that a subway would present so many advantageous aspects to them that they would be willing to pay liberally for its lease.

An undertaking of such magnitude involving an expenditure of great sums of money, as it would, must necessarily be approached with caution and decided upon only after a most thorough investigation and consideration of its manifold features, and a thoroughly and definitely expressed understanding between the parties in interest. But if it should be deemed feasible and desirable, no time should be wasted in taking the preliminary steps.

. . .

MUNICIPAL OWNERSHIP

The public ownership of public utilities is a question of public policy that has been widely discussed and to some extent experimented with in this country, with varying results. I confess to a strong prejudice, on general grounds, in favor of the municipalization of some of the services now supplied to the public by private corporations. But there are certain difficulties in the way of all such enterprises, and each community finds it necessary to consider the strictly local conditions before embarking upon the experiment.

The chief obstacle encountered is how to remove a department of this character entirely from political control, not for a year or two, but for all time, and make it impossible to convert it into a dispensary of partizan favors. America's municipalities have been subjected to excessive over-charges, contract violations and inadequate service by public utility corporations to an extent to exasperate the public mind and prepare it to accept almost any kind of an experiment, however doubtful, as a means of relief. Our own city has had these experiences and many of Newark's citizens are inclined to a policy not too expensive, that promises a permanent remedy.

It is, however, wise business policy for a city to proceed cautiously with changes which must necessarily result in the expenditure of great sums of money and, to a certain extent, disturbance of existing conditions. A civic commission composed of eminent men representing both sides of the question has made careful investigation in Europe and, it is understood, has been unfavorably impressed with the operation of municipal ownership there, and hence is disposed to report against its adoption in this country. A number of American cities have intro-

duced, or are introducing, municipal ownership on a scale
large enough to afford conclusive demonstrations of the
success or failure of the theory. Before Newark should
be committed finally in either way, I believe it would
be well to await the result of the experiments of these
other municipalities.

                         . . .

PASSAIC PURIFICATION.

The purification of the Passaic River is a matter of
vital concern to the people of Newark and of other municipalities bordering upon that stream. The bitter
strife which prevented any effective action for many
years has at length died down and there now seems to be
substantial agreement upon the main points at issue.
There is therefore a favorable prospect that the negotia-
tions set on foot last year by committees composed of
officials and private citizens of this city and Paterson
will result in the presentation to the Legislature of a
bill to permit the building of a joint trunk sewer which
shall carry off the sewage and other refuse which now
pollute the river. To forward this great work in every
way possible is my desire and I promise every effort to
that end.

DEEPER RIVER CHANNEL.

The great prosperity and growth of Newark are largely due to the navigable river upon whose banks the city
is built. By reason of the low charges made for transportation of freight by water, Newark merchants and manufacturers are enabled to secure favorable rates from
the railroad companies for the carrying of their goods.
The commerce of the Passaic has grown to enormous pro-
portions, but must soon suffer a serious check unless
the river channel can be deepened so as to permit vessels
of large draft to come up to the city docks. Through the
enterprise of the Board of Trade the subject has been
fully and graphically presented to Congress with a plea
for an adequate appropriation for a work of such importance. While a matter of this kind lies without the province of the Mayor of the city, I take pleasure in ex-
pressing my willingness to co-operate at any time and in
any way with those who are seeking to bring about this
necessary improvement.

THE REPORT OF THE SUPERINTENDENT
OF SCHOOLS -- 1909

Excerpts from the report of the
Superintendent of Schools presented in 1909 follow.

Source: <u>Fifty-Third Annual Report of the Board of Education of Newark, N.J. for the School Year Ending June
30, 1909</u>, Newark, 1909, pp. 94-96.

POPULARIZATION OF TEMPERANCE THROUGH SCHOOL
INSTRUCTION

It is only a few years since the public schools were
practically silent on the subject of intemperance and
when little or no instruction was given concerning the
use of tobacco and other narcotics. A few noble women
appreciating the situation, sought to change it through
local appeals. This method was found to be slow and un-
satisfactory. It was found that no considerable progress
could be made except through an appeal to legislatures
to make temperance instruction mandatory. Witness the
phenomenal success of this movement! Public opinion was
worked up to a high pitch. One after another, nearly
every state in the Union adopted the legislation proposed.
That the result of this movement has been productive of
good cannot be doubted. Whatever may be said to the
contrary it must be admitted by all:
First, that it has raised the embargo of silence.
It has unshackled the lips of teachers. They no longer
fear the wrath of the interested saloonkeeper nor the
attack by the parent who uses tobacco.
Second, it has popularized total abstinence. I can
recall when among certain classes, it was an unusual act
to refuse to drink liquor with friends. "My doctor has
commanded me not to drink" was the only excuse accepted.
Non-alcoholic drinks were not generally to be found except at high class bars. Now mineral waters are kept
everywhere, even in the smallest and meanest of saloons.
I attribute this change in no small measure to the general
<u>popularization of temperance</u> through school instruction.

TEACHING OF SEX MORALITY

The success of temperance instruction in schools
leads me to think that the moral instruction now given in
our schools could safely be extended to include many important topics of sex morality. I believe a mistake has
been made in leaving to the parent all instruction of
this nature. The fact is, as we all know, that few parents are properly qualified to give such instruction,

and few ever attempt it. The boy and girl during the
period of adolescence, if not, indeed, in most cases
sooner, get all their sex notions from the lips and acts
of possibly vicious playmates or from careless and often
corrupt adults with whom they are necessarily thrown more
or less in contact. The fear that such instruction if
appropriately given will react by suggestion and lead
to consequences the opposite of those intended is to
my mind a foolish one. We have no more reason to expect it than we have to expect that every boy will smoke
cigarettes or get drunk because of our teaching the evils
of the tobacco habit and of intemperance.

If such instruction were to be given in the schools
certain things, however, would need to be guarded against.
Thus, it would not do to have instruction of this kind
given by all teachers, but only those suitably qualified
and possessing the necessary sympathy, delicacy and tact.
It would be best, it seems to me, to approach the subject from the standpoint of hygiene and not from the
standpoint of the teacher of morals. This I conceive to
be all important. The school physician, if a man and
possessing the necessary qualifications, could safely
talk to boys; or, if a woman physician, to girls. Instruction should be limited to the simplest hygienic matters such as care of body, cleanliness, exercise, food,
sleep, clothing, dangers attending over-excitement of
the imagination in reading, in attending theatres, etc.;
lessons on becoming behavior in presence of the other
sex, modesty, propriety in public and private; in fact,
nearly the whole content of appropriate sexual behav-
ior--and this without exciting an impure thought and
certainly without setting the current of emotional life
in the wrong direction. As an antidote to the flagi-
tious and highly exciting novels read by so many boys
and girls and to the erotic plays so often witnessed,
often in the presence of their parents, such instruction rightly given--which means by competent physicians speaking with the authority of the family physician as well as the pupil's friend--such instruction is abundantly needed.

A GREETING FROM NEWARK-ON-TRENT ON THE
TWO HUNDRED FIFTIETH ANNIVERSARY OF NEWARK'S
FOUNDING -- 1916

A greeting sent in March 1916 by
the officials of Newark-on-Trent,
England, to Newark, New Jersey,
on the two hundred fiftieth anniversary of the founding of the
latter follows.

Source: Framed document in the Office of the City Clerk,
Newark, New Jersey.

To the Mayor and Common Council
of the City of Newark, New Jersey,
and to the Committee of one hundred
We the Mayor and Corporation of the ancient and loy-
al Borough of Newark-on-Trent, England, in Council assembled this twenty seventh day of March one thousand nine
hundred and sixteen send heartiest greetings and felici-
tations upon the celebration of the two hundred and fiftieth anniversary of the planting of your city. We re-
joice greatly at the marvellous progress and prosperity
of the daughter city.

This Ancestor-Borough of Newark-on-Trent was known
to the Romans as "Ad Pontem" B.C. 54, and as "Oldwork"
to the Saxons in A.D. 450. The present name of Newark
was probably a corruption of New-Work, either because of
a new town built upon the ruins of the old, or because of
a new work erected in our ancient Castle here. In the
history of England this town has played a great part. It
was here the struggles of the Civil War terminated by the
surrender outside our walls of King Charles 1st.

Our Royal Charters of Incorporation date back to
1550 (Edward VI), our Mayor and Corporation to 1625
(Charles 1st), thus our present Mayor is the 291st of
his long line.

We recite these particulars as showing your City is
linked up with one of no mean origin, and it is a source
of pride to us to note the frame and importance in Art,
Education, and Manufacture which Newark, N.J. has at-
tained under your hands.

CELEBRATING THE TWO HUNDRED FIFTIETH ANNIVERSARY
OF NEWARK'S FOUNDING -- 1916

> The celebration beginning in May
> 1916 of the two hundred fiftieth
> anniversary of the founding of
> Newark took place with a variety
> of activities.

Source: Thomas L. Rayomnd, "Newark's Anniversary Celebration," The American City, XIV, May 1916, pp. 491-493.

. . . The city of Newark began on May 1 the celebration of the 250th anniversary of her founding, which will
continue for five months in a series of more than one
hundred very interesting events. This will give an opportunity to the citizens to pay due honor to the memory
of Robert Treat and the brave men who came from Connecticut and founded the little settlement on the Passaic River as the nucleus of what has become the metropolis of
New Jersey with a population of 400,000 people.
The citizens have united in a splendid effort to du-
ly commemorate this event in what will be in the truest
sense a celebration in which the entire community will
take its share. The business men of the city and others
have contributed $250,000, and at the last general elec-
tion the people voted for an issue of bonds of $1,500,000
for the erection of a permanent Memorial Building, the
corner stone of which will be laid as is now hoped during
the latter part of the celebration.
The importance of Newark in the state and in the
country, it is thought by many, has been somewhat over-
shadowed by the city of New York, which is so near us,
but this celebration will do more than anything that has
been done in the past to place Newark where she belongs
in the eyes of the people of this country. Newark is
the eleventh city in the United States in point of manufactures. There are within her borders 2,200 factories
in which 252 different varieties of goods are manufactured, of an annual value of $259,000,000.
The people of all classes--men, women and children--
have felt the stir of this great civic enterprise. En-
thusiasm for its success and activity in bringing that
success about may be found alike in the shop, the store,
the factory, the church, the school and the city government. The prominent citizens have been especially active
in making this one of the greatest of municipal celebra-
tions, not only commercially, but also in a more spiritual sense, and in combining the material life of the
community with the intellectual in such a way as to give
rise to the term "The Newark Idea."
One of the important opening events will be the

largest music festival that has been held anywhere in
the East in recent years. Thousands of singers from
three of New Jersey's largest cities, members of festival societies, will appear for six magnificent performances from the opening day, May 1 to May 4. Large prize
money and the excellent management of the Newark Music
Festival Association have resulted in creating new music
of great beauty. Band and orchestra will be massed together with an imposing list of selections by vocal artists of the Metropolitan Opera Company of New York.

Dates have been already fixed and announced for
fifty public events. Especially noteworthy will be the
Newark Industrial Exposition from May 13 to June 3, which
is to be opened by President Woodrow Wilson and which
will bring forcibly to the attention of the country the
variety and character of Newark's manufactures.

On the nights of May 30, 31 and June 1 and 2 there
will be a splendid historic pageant in Weequahic Park,
one of the most beautiful city parks. The pageant will
cost about $60,000 and will involve the dramatic ser-
vices of 3,500 persons. It is estimated that 50,000 people will view each performance. Half of the seats and
all of the standing room will be free. This pageant,
which has been written by Mr. Thomas Wood Stevens, the
eminent dramatist, must have the effect of giving a ro-
mantic touch to the city, which those who see the pageant, both old and young, will carry with them for the
rest of their lives.

Athletic events of national importance will be provided at a cost of $40,000. In the various events which
are to continue throughout the celebration in the course
of the five months, there are to be many parades, con-
ventions, special ceremonies, sports, tournaments, con-
certs, religious mass meetings, theatricals, automobile
gymkhana, and contests, military exercises, charitable
surveys and school exhibits.

An interesting feature of the celebration has been
the famous poster contest, resulting in the creation of
a splendid series of art posters of which THE AMERICAN
CITY has already published reproductions of the prize-
winning designs.

We have faith that this great celebration will place
Newark before the people of this country in her true
light; that it will awaken within her citizens a nobler
public spirit; and that it will tend to create a civic
genius which will send her forth in the splendid years
to be with new aspirations, new ideals, new hopes and a
new spirit of civic devotion and loyalty.

                                    THOMAS L. RAYMOND
                                              Mayor
                            ⎾Newark, New Jersey⏌

A NEW CONTRACT FOR GARBAGE DISPOSAL -- 1919

> An account by the engineering
> supervisor of the Bureau of
> Street Cleaning and Refuse
> Collection of a contract a-
> warded on July 3, 1919, for
> garbage disposal follows.

Source: James W. Costello, "Newark, N.J., Contracts for
Garbage Disposal," The American City, XXI, October 1919,
p. 314.

A contract for the purchase and final disposition
of garbage by feeding was awarded to the National Uti-
lization Company by the city of Newark on July 3, 1919,
for a period of five years commencing September 1, 1919.
The price to be paid to the city for each ton of garbage
delivered is eight times the price per pound of live
killing hogs on the Chicago market, as determined by
averaging the top price for each month.
      The piggery is to be located along the shore of the
Passaic River, and the city wagons are to deliver all
garbage to the feeding site, where it will be weighed.
The city agrees to the enforcement of existing ordinances,
to effect a good primary separation, and also agrees to
endeavor to pass ordinances whereby the contractor will
receive all hotel and restaurant garbage.
      The collection of all city refuse was done by con-
tract until 1916, when the contractor terminated the contract on the ground that the separation ordinance was not
enforced. The contract was then taken over and carried
on by municipal forces. For several years past there
has been a rather unsuccessful attempt to separate garbage from other refuse. In March, 1919, a new ordinance
was introduced requiring the separation of ashes, rub-
bish and garbage. At the present time separation is effective thruout the city, collection being made in refuse
wagons having separate compartments. A police officer and
inspector is assigned to each district to enforce this
ordinance, and the results have been very gratifying.
      The erection of a reduction plant of 150-ton capa-
city was contemplated, but the present cost of building
material is considered prohibitive. An estimate received
from one company was $750,000 exclusive of the cost of
the site. The city has some 6 square miles of meadow
land, and all classes of refuse have formerly been dumped
on this land. There is a contract for the salvaging of
the material, for which privilege the city receives $3,000
annually. The contractor also supplies all labor necessary to keep the dumps and the roads leading thereto in
good working condition....

THE OPENING OF THE NEWARK MUSEUM -- 1926

> In March 1926 the Newark Museum,
> which had been housed in the
> Newark Public Library, opened
> its own building.

Source: <u>Newark Star Eagle</u>, March 17, 1926.

A blaze of light flared through the huge arched windows of the big, new, white-fronted building at Washington street and Washington place early last night.

A short time later the two massive bronze doors opened, revealing a greater flood of light against bright colored within, and then through the doors began to flow a steady stream of humanity.

An hour after the doors had swung open, over 3,000 persons had entered. All stayed to witness the formal opening of Newark's new shrine of art, science and industry. Men in formal dress, women in evening gown, others in plain business clothes were there. The rich and the poor alike, rubbed elbows, for theirs was a common cause--love for the beautiful.

Place Crowded

The occasion was the formal opening of the new $700,000 building of the Newark Museum, with its $1,000,000 collection of rare and beautiful objects. And the visitors included not only art lovers of Newark and immediate vicinity, but notables from New York and other cities.

Long before the time set for the address of Mayor Raymond, the speaker of the evening, the sunken, skylighted court was filled to overflowing. Likewise, the crowd surged about the main hall into which the visitors enter directly from the street. As time advanced, the rest of the first floor exhibition rooms were filled and many of those who could not find seats or advantageous standing room went up to look at the Leather Exhibit on the second floor, while others ascended to the third floor which houses the science department.

The museum's policy of encouraging modern American painters, expressed in its collection of 23 works by leaders in the American art field, was the basis of enthusiastic comment. Many persons, art lovers, critics and students, came from all over the metropolitan district to view the collection, which had been purchased during the past year and which was put on display last night for the first time. . . .

Donor Absent

Arthur F. Egner, in the absence of Wallace M. Scudder, president of the Newark Museum Association, was chairman. After briefly outlining the objects and aims of the museum, Mr. Egner expressed regret that Louis Bamberger, donor of the museum to the city, was unable to be present at the opening ceremonies. However, he read a telegram from Mr. Bamberger in Florida deploring his inability to attend.

After lauding Mr. Bamberger and John Cotton Dana, director of the museum since it was founded seventeen years ago, Mr. Egner introduced Mayor Raymond, the principal speaker of the evening. In his address, the complete text of which will be found elsewhere, Mayor Raymond outlined what the Newark Museum stands for in the life of the city and what it means to education and industry in Newark.

The museum, Mayor Raymond said, "is to be a museum of fine arts, an industrial museum and a museum of science, and yet, art is as much a basis of the industrial side as of the department of fine arts."

In the audience, aside from prominent residents of Newark and suburbs, were art lovers of national repute from New York and other cities. Included among these were: Mary Gibson of the Museum of Decorative Arts, New York; Edward Forbes of Harvard University, Robert P. Fischelis of Washington, Frederick L. Lewton of the Smithsonian Institute, Keith Zwar of Melbourne, Australia, here studing leather, and John Flanagan of New York, who made the bronze relief of Mr. Bamberger which hangs in the main corridor.

Besides out-of-town visitors, Mr. Dana received telegrams and letters of congratulation on the opening of the museum from all parts of the country. These included messages from Frederick A. Whitney, director of the Cleveland Museum; Dr. Sao Ke Alfred Sze, Chinese Ambassador at Washington; Richard F. Bach of the Metropolitan Museum of Art, New York; the Tennessee Historical Society of Nashville, Tenn.; the Pennsylvania Museum, Fairmont Park, Pa.; Homer Eaton Keyes of Boston, Mass.; Ernest Martin Hopkins, president of Dartmouth College; John M. Thomas of Rutgers University; Arthur MacLean, director of the John Herron Art Institute, Indianapolis; the Charleston Museum of Charleston, S. C., and others.

Others who sent congratulations from all parts of the county are: Charles Belden, president of the American Library Association, Chicago; Owen Moon, Jr., publisher of the Winston-Salem Journal, Winston-Salem, N. C.; Miss Julia B. Douglas, Evergreen, Col., and Howard L. Hughes, librarian of the Trenton Public Library.

The panorama of exhibits which greeted the eyes of the public last night was a sight of rare beauty. On

entering the main hall from the door on Washington
street, visitors were ushered into a huge center room
with row after row of neatly arranged glass cases containing exhibits. In the center of the large skylighted
court stands the exact model of the Venus de Milo, gleam-
ing against a blue background, at its furthest side.

To the right of the main hall, as the visitors enter, is a room containing the new exhibit of the works of
living American artists. This collection was secured
during the past year and was shown for the first time
publicly at the opening last night. It contains a score
or more of the paintings of well-known and a few capable
but obscure American artists.

Great Artists

This collection, which presents the first fruits of
the museum's avowed policy to encourage contemporary A-
merican art, includes works by Robert Henri, John Sloan,
George Luks, Jerome Myers, George Bellows, William J.
Glackens, Gifford Beal, Louis Kronberg, Guy Pene Du Bois,
Samuel Halpert, Louise Upton Brumback, Bryson Burroughs,
Augustus Vincent Tack, Arthur B. Wilder, Joseph Pollet,
Grave Ravlin and Niles Spencer.

Next to the American artists' collection is the museum office. From the main center room, other exhibit
rooms are visible through arched doorways. Around the
other side of the court is the Oriental exhibit, in which
selections from Tibet, Korea, China and Japan are shown.
Next to this comes the children's museum, containing a
bountiful supply of things nearest kiddies' hearts, models of Eskimos and their homes, Indians, their weapons,
pictures and statues of characters famous in American
history.

One of the features of the children's musuem is the
lending department, which sends out exhibits to schools
and educational institutions. During the past year this
department furnished nearly 2,000 individual exhibits a
month to Newark schools. These cover a wide range including industrial subjects from asbestos to zinc; miner-
als, from agate to petrified wood, and objects illus-
trating the customs of the races of men; insect life,
bird life and countless other subjects.

One of the chief objects of the museum is to be a
workshop of education and an assistant to all educational
activity of the city. The lending department includes
examples of Newark's industrial activities, products
from its factories and workshops, including textiles,
leather, varnish, celluloid, pottery and varnish.

On the second floor, in neatly arranged cases and
on tables and stands, is the big leather exhibit, one of
the finest ever shown in America. It includes specimens
of the leather industry throughout the world....

A SALARY REDUCTION FOR THE NEWARK
PUBLIC LIBRARY STAFF -- 1932

In June 1932 the Newark Library
staff agreed to take a reduction
in salary because of the Depression.

Source: <u>Newark Evening News</u>, June 13, 1932.

The 243 employees of the Newark Free Public Library
have agreed to take a 10 per cent cut in salary for the
year beginning July 1, the library's board of trustees
was informed at its monthly meeting this afternoon.

Members of the board are in favor of the reduction
and will notify Mayor Congleton to that effect. The city
furnishes most of the money with which the main library
and its eight branches are operated, though the actual
administration of the library system is vested in the
board of trustees, which is not directly responsible to
the City Commission.

The library employees are under Civil Service. They
are the first public employees in Newark to accept a reduction in salary. Their agreement to a pay cut came
after some members of the staff had agreed to much heav-
ier sacrifices if this is necessary to keep the libraries open. Miss Beatrice Winser, librarian and secretary
of the library board, agreed to a 20 per cent reduction
in her salary rather than have some of the lesser paid
workers cut.

This year's library budget is $556,000 of which
$354,000 is for salaries. Virtually all of this is sup-
plied by Newark, though the library has an endowment of
about $20,000, the interest from which is used to add to
the book collection. As an offset against the appropriation given by Newark, the library returns to the city
the $25,000 to $30,000 collected in fines.

Lathrop Anderson, president of the board, announced
the agreement of the employees in a statement made public
at today's meeting. His statement disclosed that Mayor
Congleton had suggested that instead of a flat 10 per
cent cut, there be a graduated scale.

Mr. Congleton's plan, which he favors for application to all city employees, would call for no city cuts
on salaries under $1,000. Those of $1,000 to $2,000
would be cut 2 per cent. Those from $2,000 to $3,000
would be cut 7½ per cent. Those from $3,000 to $5,000
would be cut 10 per cent. Those from $5,000 to $10,000
would be cut 12½ per cent and all above $10,000, 15 per
cent.

Mr. Anderson's statement declared:
"Week before last the mayor explained to me the ne-

cessity for a cut in wages for all city employees. He
asked if our board of trustees would consider such a
proposition. A week ago Friday Miss Beatrice Winser, who
is secretary of the library, called a meeting of the
heads of each department of the library. I explained to
them the present condition of the city's finances, making
the statement that the money to pay salaries comes from
the pockets of the property owners. If these people cannot pay their taxes because their tenants are out of work,
with no money to pay rents, the income of the city is
lowered. Therefore, some way must be found to reduce
expenses.

"I suggested to the staff at the time that they all
accept a cut of 10 per cent for one year. I also stated
if the city was unable to collect enough money to run the
government we might have to close some of the departments,
including the library.

"After I had answered numerous questions and there
had been considerable discussion, one patriotic young lady said it would be a pity to close the library or any
of its departments at the present time because so many
people are coming to the library to consult scientific
and medical books and also studying other books to learn
to improve their chances of getting better situations
when business improves.

"She remarked that while none of them relishes reduced salaries, she had been able to save a little money
and would be willing to work this year for no salary rather than have the library closed.

"Our secretary, who has charge of our library and
all its branches, said many of our younger girls are
earning only $15 a week and, rather than have their week-
ly check reduced by 10 per cent, she would volunteer to
have her salary reduced 20 instead of 10 per cent.

"After learning the reason for the mayor's suggestion, the entire group was absolutely patriotic in a-
greeing to do what they could to help the mayor and the
taxpayers get the city on a sound financial basis 'with
the hope that by this time next year we will all be able
to return to normal conditions.' When asked by Miss
Winser if they understood my proposal and if they were
willing to accept it, every one in the room raised her
hand."

Mr. Anderson said the mayor's graduated scale of reductions had not yet been put up to the library employees,
but that this would be done.

THE NEW PENNSYLVANIA RAILROAD STATION -- 1935

In March 1935 the new Pennsylvania
Railroad Station was dedicated.

Source: <u>Newark Evening News</u>, March 23, 1935.

The Pennsylvania Railroad's new $20,000,000 station
project, marking a new era in Newark's transportation
history, was the Mecca today of thousands attending the
formal dedication.

Completion consummated, the first of three major
parts of the extensive improvements in which the city,
the railroad and Public Service Co-ordinated Transport,
are engaged at an estimated cost of $42,000,000.

The subsequent major parts are the City Railway,
nearing completion for operation of sub-surface trolley
cars through the heart of the city and further railroad
improvements. These include enlargement of the station,
addition of five tracks to the three already constructed,
and the extension of the Hudson & Manhattan Tube tracks
to South street through the new station.

ACTUAL OPERATION TOMORROW

Actual railroad operation of the station will start
tomorrow at 10:17 A. M., when the New York-Philadelphia
express will stop westbound for Newark passengers. Thereafter every Pennsylvania train will stop in the station.

Today's program was divided into two parts, reception of 1,400 invited guests and dedication of the station between 1 and 3:30 o'clock and opening of the station to the public after 4 o'clock.

The first train into the station will arrive at 2:45
this afternoon and will be a special from New York bringing railroad, public and civic officials who are taking
part in the formal ceremonies.

The guests invited for the exercises include leading
citizens in Newark and vicinity, heads of civic and business organizations and leaders in the professions. They
arrived between 12:30 and 1 o'clock, to partake of a
buffet luncheon in the station, inspect the structure and
attend the dedicatory exercises.

Replaces 1899 Station

The new structure replaces the old station, erected
in 1899 and enlarged in 1903. It represents the latest
word in construction for railroad purposes, with every
possible convenience and comfort for the traveling public....

THE END OF TROLLEY CAR SERVICE -- 1937

> On December 18, 1937, trolley car
> service on Broad Street, the main
> thoroughfare, was replaced by
> bus service.

Source: <u>Newark Evening News</u>, December 16, 1937.

From horse cars to buses in a century. That's the
transportation history of Broad street.

Approval by the Public Utilities Commission today
of a Public Service Co-ordinated Transport application
to substitue all-service buses for trolley cars on the
Mt. Prospect line means the end of trolleys in Broad
street Sunday. The change will be made at midnight.

It was exactly 101 years ago that the first horse-
drawn car rumbled along the street, holding sway in
good weather and bad. It was slow but it served its purpose until displaced by the arks propelled by electricity from overhead wires.

"Hold Your Horses"

First trolley cars in Broad street made their appearance in the nineties. Old timers can recall the
shock and surprise which these "modern" vehicles created.
Drivers of skittish horses had to hold stiff rein on
their animals and even a docile beast reared at sight of
one of the newfangled machines.

The end of trolley service in the city's main thoroughfare had been set for early next year. The commission decided to allow the change earlier to ease traffic conditions for Christmas shoppers in the downtown
area.

An idea of the changes from trolleys to buses may
be gained from the fact that in 1923, 300 trolley cars
an hour passed the Four Corners. Service at the curb in
buses, as against boarding and departing from trolley
cars in the center of such a wide street as Broad street,
tells the story of added safety by the change. Greater
speed by buses and more modern travel comfort are other
elements.

Still in Subway

Residents of suburban lines will be the last to use
trolley cars. These now enter Newark's center by City
Subway, however, and are no impediment to street traffic.
Sentiment in the Oranges has favored abolishment of trolleys on the Central and Orange-West Orange lines and substitution of buses. No official steps have been taken

to make the change from trolleys to buses there, however.

The Broad and Harrison lines of trolleys preceded
the departing Mt. Prospect cars last September. Other
trolley cars went out of existence in favor of buses
previously on other lines.

With departure of Broad street trolleys, Public Service can shift trolley wires from the center to the sides
of the street for use by all-service buses, operated by
electricity as well as gasoline. The new plan will benefit Public Service buses now operating in Broad street
which had to travel on gasoline there owing to the present location of the wires.

Removal of tracks and safety isles is the next step
in making additional road space available for traffic.
The city, which built the safety isles, has had several
on other streets removed as WPA projects.

The Mt. Prospect line operates from the Lake street
loop to Wolcott terrace. The route is 6.83 miles long.
The Utilities Commission, in permitting the change to
buses ruled against independent bus operators, who con-
tended substitution of buses for trolleys would mean increased service and undue competition. The independents
also maintained the application was illegal because of
the present street car franchise.

To Make 192 Daily Trips

The commission allowed the full quota of bus trips
asked by the Public Service, 192 round trips daily. The
trolley service, 125 daily round trips, included nine
trips to the Pennsylvania Station, via the City Subway.
The latter will be discontinued.

The commission also held, in granting the application, that it was obvious a substantial increase in bus
trips was necessary to meet demands of the riding public.
Buses, the ruling stated, have seating capacity 28 per
cent less than trolley cars.

Restrictions enumerated are: The 5-cent fare is continued; time schedules must be filed conforming with the
trip limitations or such modification as shall be imposed
hereafter by the commission, and all service vehicles
must be operated in strict compliance with schedules
filed.

In commenting on the decision President Bacharach of
the commission said: "The approval of the discontinuance
of the Mt. Prospect street car line carries with it the
permanent discontinuance of all trolley service on Broad
street. In a measure, this action marks a milestone in
the progress of street transportation for the City of
Newark ...."

WOR'S TWENTIETH ANNIVERSARY -- 1942

                An account of the early years of
                radio station WOR, published in
                February 1942, on the twentieth
                anniversary of its founding
                follows.

Source: <u>Sunday Call</u>, February 22, 1942.

        Twenty years ago today in a stuffy little rug-draped
room off in a corner of the furniture and "wireless" department of L. Bamberger & Co.'s store that served as its
first studio, office and transmitting site, a recording
was played of "April Showers," and a big horn-shaped microphone was pushed close to the phonograph. An engineer
operated a switch and the 250-watt reconditioned transmitter that Dr. Lee De Forrest had designed himself for
experiments with vacuum tubes announced that WOR was on
the air.
        There were no official ceremonies. Phonograph re-
cordings marked that day on the air. The De Forrest
transmitter squealed and squawked and listeners tried in
vain to catch the weak waves that radiated from the small
station erected on the employees' recreation roof atop
the store building.

                    First Bamberger Station

        But the event of WOR on February 22, 1922, was not
the real start of the Bamberger store's interest in "wireless." A young man, Louis Funke of Newark, was a sales-
man in the radio department. He rigged up a high-powered
spark transmitter which crashed out dots and dashes to
attract customers to the displays of amateur receiving
and transmitting equipment. The station was licensed
by the government to use the call letters 2AJB, with
Funke as operator.
        A few months later the spark set was dismantled and
a radiophone took its place. Funke would shout: "Hello,
Hello, 1, 2, 3, 4, 5--anyone hearing my voice please call
L. Bamberger & Co." The radiophone attracted considerable
attention and sales sky-rocketed in radio supplies. Phonograph records were played for listeners and customers
were put on the air to talk to friends.

                    Jack Poppele Joins Staff

        One of the station's experts who helped put it on
the air was Jack R. Poppele, a young man who had the title of "assistant operator." Two months later the chief

engineer, John Orvis, resigned because he said that he
didn't think the "wireless telephone" had much of a future. Poppele took over and became the chief engineer,
the post he still holds today. In 20 years he has helped
radio find its future and watched WOR grow from a small
250-watt station to the maximum power permitted in the
United States, 50,000 watts.

WOR's progress in the first few months was slow--in
fact, engineers were proud of the signals that reached
Asbury Park and other Jersey points. The Bamberger company was so enthused that it took a newspaper "ad" in the
Newark Sunday Call to tell about it.

In the first year WOR began to do big things. On
October 1, 1922 the station broadcast the first international program ever transmitted. The late Sir Thomas
Lipton delivered a message intended for England, and the
orchestra played British and American tunes. A year later WOR attempted to stretch its signals to Tokio, Japan.
Paul Whiteman's orchestra was finally reported by a cable message to have been heard there.

The night of January 18, 1924 saw one of the most
dramatic incidents in WOR's history. The station received word that the giant dirigible Shenandoah had escaped from its mooring at Lakehurst and buffeted by a
gale, had disappeared. The WOR control room picked up
an SOS signal of distress from the crew on the airship.
Listeners were asked to report to the station if they
heard the ship's motor overhead. Calls followed and WOR
was able to broadcast to the ship its location and course,
enabling it to return safely home. For that service WOR
received official commendation from the U. S. Navy.

Sunday Call on WOR

The Sunday Call played an important part in the
early days of WOR with a children's program called the
"Man in the Moon" told by the late William F. B. McNeal
and Albert E. Sonn, and radio technical talks by the
latter, all of which were on the air for about a year
and a half.

Alfred J. McCosker, formerly of the Sunday Call advertising staff, joined WOR as its first publicity director. He was also in charge of special events. McCosker
became manager of WOR in 1926 and in 1933 was made president, the position which he still holds. WOR is the key
station in the metropolitan area for the Mutual Broad-
casting System.

TRAFFIC CONTROL -- 1946

An account by the director of public safety of traffic control in
Newark in November 1946 follows.

Source: John B. Keenan, "Catching Up on Traffic Control,"
LXI, The American City, November 1946, p. 114.

Newark, in northern New Jersey and adjacent to New
York City, is not only the metropolis and greatest retail center of the state but is also the geographical
center of the richest and most populous section of the
United States. Its location and its great airport, ship-
ping port, federal and state highways and largest coordi-
nated system of coach service in America, have all contributed to making traffic control and facilitation a
top problem.

Traffic congestion is not only bad for tempers and
business, an ever-present discomfort and danger, but it
exacts a startling economic toll in the form of accidents.
These cost on the average about $3,000,000 per year--
against $650,000 for fire losses.

Ask a Newark citizen what's the solution for traffic
congestion and he's likely to answer: traffic signals.
While this is far from the whole story, we do have General Electric signals on the four corners of 200 intersec-
tions. All were installed on the basis of actual conditions and accident history. For the last three years
we have mounted them 15 feet to light center instead of
9 feet as formerly. They are suspended horizontally from
ornamental brackets on Union Metal standards. For ser-
vicing them, we have just purchased one of the new tower
lift trucks made by the American Coach and Body Company
of Cleveland. Incidentally, we purchased this device from
an advertisement in The American City without even seeing
a manufacturer's representative.

Automatic Traffic Control

The controlling element of the central traffic control panel in the Traffic Engineering Bureau in City Hall
is an I.B.M. master time clock, and program devices which
provide for daily changes in the traffic control system
automatically adjust intersection controllers and provide total cycle changes and flash-off adjustments as
scheduled. A G-E supervising timer maintains system
traffic progression plan.

On August 27, 1946, all U-turns were abolished in
the central business district. In September, thirteen
40- to 50-foot streets in a congested area embracing several secondary business districts were made one-way....

THE ADOPTION OF THE MAYOR-COUNCIL
FORM OF GOVERNMENT -- 1953

On November 3, 1953, the mayor-
council form of government supplanted the commission form.

Source: Benjamin Baker, "Newark Gets a Modern City Charter," The American City, LXIX, February 1954, pp. 106-
107.

An interesting experiment in municipal government
has just taken place in New Jersey. Citizens of Newark,
New Jersey's most populous municipality, disgusted with
36 years of commission government, voted to scrap it in
favor of the mayor-council type.

The law under which charter revision has been carried out is the Optional Municipal Charter Law of 1950,
more popularly known as the Faulkner Act. Under this
statute, municipalities desiring to change their form
of government are offered a wide range of choice.

Three basic charters--the mayor-council, council-
manager, and the small municipalities plan--in 15 ver-
sions are available. Differences in the plans are largely related to such matters as the number of councilmen,
concurrent or overlapping terms of office, ward repre-
sentation, and the use of partisan or nonpartisan elections.

Citizens of a municipality who desire to change
their form of government may employ either the process of
direct petition and referendum or a charter commission to
study the existing form of government and make recommendations for change. If the second alternative is adopted,
then the proposal for a study of the government and the
selection of a charter commission must be submitted to
the people for their approval.

In Newark the movement for charter revisions began
in January, 1953. In the middle of that month, Leo Carlin, then Director of Public Works, announced that he
favored a study of the city's governmental structure.
Characterizing the commission form as a "splinter system of government," Mr. Carlin called upon the city commission to authorize an election in May 1953 on the question: "Shall a charter commission be elected to study
the charter of the city of Newark and to consider a new
charter or improvements in the present charter and to
make recommendations thereon?"

At approximately the same time the Newark Citizens'
Committee on Municipal Government, organized four years
earlier to obtain support for the passage of the Faulkner
Act, announced at a public meeting that it would solicit
signatures for a referendum to study the form of govern-

ment, and that it would nominate candidates for the proposed charter commission.

The Carlin motion, laid aside for two weeks was considered by the city commission on February 4. After a heated debate, the proposal to put the charter referendum study on the ballot was defeated by a three to two vote.

Citizens' Committee Activated

The failure of the governing body to act favorably left the field largely to the citizens' committee. It chose a five-man slate for the charter commission and launched an intensive drive to obtain the legally required number of signatures in support of both its nominees and the charter referendum.

Volunteer teams composed of civic, labor, professional, and business groups, conducted a door-to-door campaign, solicited signatures on the streets of downtown Newark, and even boarded buses at various points to ask citizens to sign petitions. Assisted by a favorable press, the campaign more than justified the hopes of its sponsors.

In the weeks that followed the NCCMG sought to educate the citizenry to the need for a nonpartisan study of their government. Public acceptance was gradual but definite. In March four candidates for election to the city commission expressed themselves in favor of putting the charter referendum on the ballot. On May 12 a total of 63,151 votes were cast in favor of the question; only 8,189 votes were recorded in opposition. The five-member charter commission slate sponsored by the NCCMG was also elected by a substantial majority.

Within a few days after its election, the charter commission was ready to begin work. It selected Alan V. Lowenstein as chairman, obtained an allotment of money from the governing body, and hired five consultants to assist it in making a study of the governmental structure of Newark.

Charter Commission's Procedure

In the light of subsequent charges made by its opponents, it is of interest to note that the charter commission took itself seriously. Individual conferences were held with the newly elected city commissioners. Seven public hearings were conducted either at City Hall or in various neighborhoods. Informal meetings were convened with organized groups representing all shades of opinion within the city. Field surveys were made to Hartford, Boston, and Philadelphia.

In August the charter commission issued a preliminary report for the consideration of the citizens. In it

tentative decisions were set forth and the people were
asked to give their advice. On September 3, the charter
commission issued its final conclusions.

The final report constitued a severe indictment of
the commission government. Municipal government in Newark, in the words of the charter study group, was "waste-
ful, extravagant, uncoordinated, and not responsive to
the needs of our city."

Low civic pride and morale was found to exist among
city employees. Five governments instead of one were in
operation, and as a result, the city was deprived of the
opportunity for effective leadership. Throughout its report stress was placed upon the need for unified action,
coordination of services and a higher standard of performance of the city's business.

Strong Mayor-Administrator Form Recommended

The charter commission recommended that the voters
adopt a strong mayor-administrator form of government,
with a mayor responsible for policy leadership and a
business manager in charge of the details of budget, personnel, and purchase. The governing body was to consist
of a council of nine, five of whom were to be elected on
the basis of newly created wards.

The ink was hardly dry on the report when the political brickbats began to fly. Wild charges and appeals
to all sections of the community were made, in the effort
to keep the old form of government.

Supporters of the charter reform were quick to re-
spond. Civic groups, organized labor and independent citizens rallied to its side. Such groups as the Taxpayers
Protective League, the City Council, the Municipal Managers League, and the Young Democrats joined with many
other organizations in announcing their support of charter revision.

The Newark Citizens' Committee on Municipal Government, principal proponent of charter change, continued
its effective campaign of personal contact with the
voter.

In the November elections a stinging rebuke was administered to the opposition. Newark citizens by a 2-1
voted adopted the recommendations of the Charter Commission for a strong mayor-administrator type of government.

Thus the first barrier has been hurdled. Newark now
has an instrument of government more in line with advanced municipal practice. Next May a new government
will be chosen. Effective government requires capable
people. To complete the governmental reform Newark citizens now must choose officials of whom they can be
justly proud.

A NEWARK EXPOSITION -- 1956

> In February 1956 the city held an
> exposition in which products rep-
> resenting its economic and civic
> activities were displayed.

Source: <u>Newark Evening News</u>, February 4, 1956.

Brimming with pride, an old lady, who just recently
has been gaining the respect she deserves, stepped out
and took a bow last night at Sussex Avenue Armory.

The City of Newark, in the opening night of a week-
long exposition, displayed attributes which both en-
lightened and delighted the crowd of more than 8,100
who viewed the show.

In all of the 100 exhibits--which form a representative display of the city's industrial, business, civic
and official life--there are notes of pride in accomplishments, and of confidence in the future.

"There's a new NEW in Newark," proclaims the city
Chamber of Commerce, which is co-sponsor of the show
with the Mayor's Committee for Economic Development.
The slogan is backed up in the displays.

Building Boom Shown

The city's 100-million-dollar building boom is de-
picted in models and sketches of the new structures.

Displays of various city departments and agencies
portray the part they play in keeping the life blood of
Newark moving. They reflect the change in form of city
government.

"Newark on Parade," as the exhibition is called,
illustrates the industrial giant which has grown from
the little settlement which Robert Treat founded on the
banks of the Passaic in 1661.

The list of products Newark's factories pour forth
is varied and long. Some are well-publicized and others
little known.

Many Things

There are pencils and platinum; beer and bread; meat
products and hot dog making machines; cardboard boxes
and electric light bulbs; valves and pumps; elastic bands
and erasers to name but a few.

Newark's banks offer visitors an opportunity to test
their abilities in detecting differences between counter-
feit and legitimate money. The city's insurance companies show in their displays the role they play in Newark.

An exhibit of The Newark News illustrates how a

modern newspaper is printed. There are photograph trans-
mitters and receivers, a teletype machine, and type, mat
and casting of a front page.

Well Guarded Display

Examples of platinum and other precious metal products are displayed by Englehard Industries. A display
case holds more than $15,000 worth of jewelry and prod-
ucts made of precious materials used in industry. The
display will be guarded 24 hours a day.

Pork is displayed by John Engelhorn & Sons in the
manner they prepare it for table use and in the live
state--in the form of two sucklings, weighing 30 pounds
apiece and 2 months old.

You can ring a bell at the Prudential Insurance Co.
booth if you can answer correctly, true or false, statements like: "Whooping cough is seldom fatal."

Bamberger's display depicts the growth of the store
and the part it has played in city's business life.

Diversity

Models and photographs of the Port of New York Authority illustrate the development and projected construction at Port Newark and Newark Airport. An Urban
League exhibit reminds visitors that manpower is our
most precious resource.

At Krueger Brewing Co.'s booth, persons may sign up
for the Ground Observer Corps, which has a station atop
the Krueger plant, or for service with the Newark Welfare
Federation.

Brenner Desk Co. has an ultra-modern $7,000 desk.
It's said to do everything but think for the hard-pressed
businessman.

Sausage Stuffers

Linker Machines, Inc., has on display devices which
make frankfurters or sausages, and which take off the
cellophane casing to make them skinless.

Fine cutlery products are displayed by J. Wiss &
Sons, and Western Electric has eight telephones in color.
Making of a telephone line and solderless connections
in equipment are demonstrated.

An electronic device which can instantly tell an
airplane pilot how far he is from a landing field, and a
licensed, operating two-way radio installed in a child's
toy automobile are at the Federal Telephone and Radio
Co. exhibit....

THE CLOSING OF BURLESQUE -- 1957

In February 1957 the city's two
burlesque theaters were closed
by court action.

Source: <u>Newark Evening News</u>, February 6, 1957.

Newark soon will be a city without a burlesque
house. Minsky's announced today that it will suspend
performances indefinitely tomorrow night. The Empire
Theater said it would close its doors on Feb. 14.

Spokesmen for both theaters emphasized that the
closings will be for indefinite periods. Whether the
shows ever reopen, they added, depends on the outcome
of the court battle the theaters are waging to knock out
anti-burlesque amendments to the city theater ordinance.

The amendments, which were upheld last November by
the State Supreme Court, have resulted in the arrests of
21 burlesque performers in the last two weeks. Chief
Magistrate Nicholas Castellano today set next Friday as
the hearing date for the latest group of 11 to be arrested. All 11 were continued in $25 bail each after Cas-
tellano agreed to a postponement of the hearing requested
by the performers' attorney.

A hearing for the other 10 will be held next Wednesday.

Attendance Dwindles

Sources close to both theaters expressed some doubt
that they would reopen. They cited steadily dwindling
attendance at the shows stemming from the continuing
crackdown by police against burlesque, as a major factor.

It also is certain that, if convictions result from
any of the 21 arrests, the city would either move to revoke the licenses of the theaters immediately or would
refuse to renew them this year. The license for Minsky's
expires May 15 and for the Empire on Aug. 15.

Layoff Notices

Harold Minsky, who brought burlesque to the old Adams Theater in August 1953, said the 50 permanent employes at the theater had received one-week layoff no-
tices. He said tomorrow night's last show, beginning at
10 o'clock, would ring down the curtain.

"We can't operate," Minsky commented, "until we know
on what legal grounds we stand."

Minsky estimated that Newark now is one of only 15
to 20 cities in the country where burlesque shows operate.
The Hudson Theater in Union City, where anti-burlesque

amendments similar to Newark's were passed. will shut
down Saturday.

Henry H. Rubenson, attorney for the Empire, which
is the city's senior burlesque spot by many years, said
the theater would bring in one more change of top performers before suspending. The last show will begin
Friday and continue for a week through the night of Feb.
14.   The Empire is operated by I. Hirst Enterprises, Inc

Rubenson insisted that the suspension of performances was not intended by either theater as an admission
of guilt.

"We maintain our shows are in conformity with the
law," he declared, "but until the matter is finally ad-
judicated, we have no way of establishing our position."

Rubenson said he would continue to press the appeal
of both theaters to the United States Supreme Court to
override the decision of New Jersey's high court and declare the amendments unconstitutional.

Also pending, he stated, is a request to the State
Supreme Court to stay the mandate and enforcement of the
amendment until the appeal to the U.S. Supreme Court is
resolved.

Rubenson also served notice that, if the 21 burlesque
performers are convicted of violating the ordinance, the
theaters would take one test case and appeal it to the
State Supreme Court.

A hearing for the first group of 10 strip-tease
dancers and two male comedians arrested last week is
scheduled for next Wednesday before Magistrate Castellano.

THE NAMING OF A HOUSING PROJECT -- 1959

In October 1959 a new low income
housing project was named for
Stella Windsor Wright, a black
leader in social work.

Source: <u>Newark Star-Ledger</u>, October 15, 1959.

The new 1,200-unit Spruce St. low cost housing project was named yesterday for the late Stella Windsor
Wright, Newark leader in social work among Negroes and
founder of the Friendly Neighborhood House.

The Newark Housing Authority unanimously approved
the designation as a memorial to a woman whose "vision
and courage" established the Neighborhood House as the
first vital step toward improvement in the old Third
Ward.

Housing Commissioner Theodore P. Pettigrew, chairman of the nominating committee, said the new project
was the culmination of Mrs. Wright's efforts.

Mrs. Wright was selected for the honor after consideration of many Negro leaders including scientist
George Washington Carver; and Ebenezer Basset, Minister
to Haiti.

A REDEVELOPMENT PROJECT IN THE CENTRAL WARD
-- 1965

>   In February 1965 the Central Plan-
>   ning Board adopted a plan for a
>   redevelopment project in a twen-
>   ty-four-block area in the Central
>   Ward.

Source: <u>Newark Evening News</u>, February 16, 1965.

The Central Planning Board yesterday adopted a land
reuse plan for the Central Ward urban renewal project
that calls primarily for light industrial redevelopment
in a 24-block area now containing a large mixture of low-
grade, non-conforming uses.

The plan also provides for the expansion of existing
industries, such as the General Electric Co. plant in
17th Avenue; for expansion of school and other public
facilities; for replacement of run-down housing with new
high-rise and low-rise apartments, and for neighborhood
shopping facilities.

The land reuse plan submitted yesterday covers a
24-block area surrounded by Belmont, Avon and 17th avenues and Bergen Street. George Chranewycz, assistant
director of urban renewal for the Newark Housing Authority, said there are no present plans for industrial redevelopment south of Avon Avenue at this time.

The land reuse plan was drawn by the Newark Housing
Authority which is the city's official redevelopment
agency.

Properties Excluded

All properties in the project area will be acquired
for clearance and redevelopment except the following:
Felix Fuld housing project.
General Electric Co.
New York Bay Railroad Co. right of way.
Hayes Park West Pool.
Ricciardi Paint Co.
St. Stanislaus Church and School, 18th Avenue School,
Cleveland Junior High School and related facilities.

The area is served by the New York Bay Railroad Co.
which was built in the 1890s. The General Electric plant,
which has an annual payroll of $5 million and receives
more than 1,200 carloads of material via the railroad,
will be retained and provisions have been made in the
plan for GE expansion to the west of its present facility.

GE Expansion

The plant will undergo an expansion program according to redevelopment officials, thus making it possible
to keep industry in Newark. Ricciardi, Inc., a large
paint retailer and wholesaler, also will be given the
opportunity to expand its facilities.

The following major reuses are proposed for the
area: Residential high-density (high rise apartments),
residential medium density (low-rise), community commercial, light industrial and public and semi-public.

The community commercial area would include retail
and service establishments for the sale of goods and personal services that make up a neighborhood shopping center. The light industrial areas would restrict the use
of the land to industries such as packaging. The public
uses would include schools, playgrounds, pools and a
board of education warehouse and distribution facility to
replace one that was razed by urban renewal in Coes
Place. Semi-public uses would include churches and religious educational institutions.

The maximum land coverage by the buildings in industrial redevelopment shall not exceed 60 per cent of the
lot area, and no building shall exceed a height of 40
feet. There shall be one parking space provided for every
five employes, and one off-street loading area for each
15,000 square feet of gross leasable shall not exceed
90. This type of reuse has been designated for the
block bounded by Belmont and Waverly Avenues and Rose and
Livingston Streets.

Residential medium density shall not exceed 39 units
per acre, with this type of redevelopment scheduled for
portions of the blocks bounded by Bergen Street and Waverly and 18th avenues and by 18th and 17th avenues and
Hunterdon Street. Only 9 per cent of the dwellings in
the 24-block area were found to be owner-occupied,
according to the housing authority. The remaining residential structures are owned by absentee landlords.

Subject to Approval

The planning board's recommendation now must go before the City Council for concurrence. The housing authority must hold a public hearing before any land is
acquired, but this is merely for informational purposes.
The planning board's recommendation states that the plan
submitted yesterday is in line with the city's proposed
Master Plan.

The vote yesterday was 6-0-1 with John F. Shine,
planning board chairman, abstaining····

COLONNADE PARK'S FIFTH ANNIVERSARY -- 1965

An account of Colonnade Park, a
middle income project, published
in July 1965 on the fifth anniversary of its opening follows.

Source: <u>New York Herald Tribune</u>, July 4, 1965.

Colonnade Park, group of three 24-story buildings
in downtown Newark, N.J., containing 1,250 apartments, is
marking its fifth anniversary with 96 per cent of the
suites occupied. It has become a major commuting community for New Yorkers, with about half of the residents
working in New York City and 25 per cent being former
New York residents. It also has overcome a number of
apparent obstacles.

"Colonnade Park had a number of problems when it was
started," explained James Desdunes, resident manager of
the Newark group. It was announced as an urban renewal
project which would create luxury apartments in an area
which had no experience with luxury housing.

Moreover, the blueprint by the architect, Mies van
der Rohe, specified facades entirely of glass, an un-
tried architectural approach in the East at the time.
Thus, Colonnade Park was slated to pioneer a new architectural concept and introduce luxury apartment living
in an area unused to the idea.

A third threat to the success of the project in-
volved the City of Newark. The city was in the midst of
a vast economic and architectural revival. But, the "New
Newark" program was in its earliest years. Fortunately,
Newark's progress was obvious not only to local people
but also to New Yorkers who crossed the river to live in
Colonnade Park and now comprise about 25 per cent of
Newark's tenant population.

"The rental record to date destroys all doubts, past,
present and future about Colonnade Park's place on the real
estate and construction honor roll," asserts Mr. Desdunes.

Apprehension resulting from the revolutionary struc-
tural concept has been largely dissipated by an intelli-
gent information program, explains Mr. Desdunes. Fear of
height is non-existent, as tenants have gotten used to
the floor-to-ceiling windows and proudly display the
striking urban views to visiting friends.

Efforts to give tenants a community feeling have
paid off, according to the resident manager. The tenant
relations program is one of the most comprehensive ever
developed and is supervised by a full-time activities
director.

There are classes for dancing, gymnastics, painting,
music, and other hobbies. Teams have been formed for

bowling, bridge, skiing and softball, besides other
sports. There is a nursery school on the premises, a-
long with a snack bar, teenagers' recreation room and a
fully-furnished tenants' lounge. Personalized touches
include bulletin boards and even hair dryers for the
woman of the house.

The community-conscious owners of Colonnade Park
have set aside groups of apartments for students, teachers, doctors and nurses so that the colony is balanced
and meets the housing needs of the Newark community. Because of the nine to ten-month scholastic year of students, Colonnade Park has special summer month rentals
for many student apartments.

CELEBRATING THE THREE HUNDREDTH ANNIVERSARY
OF NEWARK'S FOUNDING -- 1966

> The celebration beginning in January
> 1966 of the three hundredth anniver-
> sary of the founding of Newark took
> place with a variety of activities.

Source: <u>Newark Evening News</u>, January 2, 1966.

A congratulatory message has been received from
President Lyndon B. Johnson commemorating the opening
of the 300th anniversary of Newark, which will continue
throughout 1966.

Briefly recounting the city's history, the President said:

"The story of Newark is America's story. It is the
story of colonization, independence, growth and maturity.
It is the story of a brave people."

Adding that it "is gratifying to know that in celebrating an eventful past, citizens of Newark are forging
new paths to civic betterment," Johnson extended wishes
for a "happy and prosperous" fourth century.

Others Laud Event

Gov. Richard J. Hughes, Mayor Hugh J. Addonizio,
Frederick H. Groel, president of the Newark 300th Anniversary Corp., and Milford A. Vieser, an honorary co-
chairman of the corporation and president of the Greater
Newark Chamber of Commerce, also issued statements marking the occasion.

No formal ceremonies have as yet been conducted.
The official anniversary celebration is scheduled for
May 18, Newark's Founders Day, the date in 1866 on which
the first settlers, led by Robert Treat, are believed to
have arrived here from Connecticut.

However, informal observation of the anniversary
began Friday with a luncheon at Continental House, celebration headquarters at 2 Park Place. Guests of honor
were Mr. and Mrs. Sandford M. Treat, both direct descendants of Robert Treat.

William F. Tompkins of Maplewood and his sister, Mrs.
Milton O. Lange of Short Hills, both descendants of Micah
Tompkins, another of the original settlers, also were
among the dozen persons attending the luncheon.

Gifts Exchanged

Groel, on behalf of the anniversary corporation and
the New Jersey Historical Society, of which he is a
trustee, presented the Treats a book from the society's
collection. The volume contains records of the town of

Newark from the time it was settled in 1666 until 1836,
when the community was incorporated as a city.

Mr. and Mrs Treat, in turn, presented Groel an original deed to property in Connecticut, bearing a rare example of Robert Treat's signature.

. . .

Gov. Hughes in his commemorative statement declared
that the anniversary celebration will emphasize "the vital role of all our central cities in relation to those
surrounding communities which utilize city resources
and services.

"As we share benefits," he said, "so must we also
partcipate, where we can, in solutions to common problems."

Governor's Pledge

The governor mentioned that the state government
will develop a new mechanism, the Department of Community Affairs, to help cities like Newark meet the "numerous challenges of modern societies." He added that he
believes that "Newark's 300th birthday is a proper time
for all of us to redeclare our faith in the life and
future of our cities."

Mayor Addonizio cited the celebration goals which
have been set forth by the Newark 300th Anniversary Corp.

They are to promote among Newark citizens, particularly among young people, a greater awareness of the
city's resources and traditions; to promote among those
who work in Newark a greater appreciation of the city's
assets; to promote the establishment of new cultural
institutions and activities, and to instill in all who
live or work here a deep sense of pride in Newark.

"People of each and every group -- economic, religious, racial, neighborhood or whatever else -- can find
common cause in the pursuit of the objectives," the Mayor
declared. "I know of no better way to unite the people
of all elements within Newark than by joining together
in the celebration."

Groel urged "universal participation" in all the
anniversary events, most of which will take place on or
after Founders Day. However, the first of the cultural
events slated for 1966 will be a series of eight performances this week by the Metropolitan Opera National
Company at Newark's Symphony Hall.

. . .

In his message Vieser asserted that, "we will dedi-
cate all our energy and resources to rebuilding our city
physically and spiritually."

Speaking as Chamber of Commerce president, he gave
assurance that the "participation and support of Newark's
business community in the 300th anniversary program will
be extensive, sincere and enthusiastic."

RIOTING -- 1967

                From July 13 to 18, 1967, riots in
                Newark resulted in twenty-three
                deaths, approximately twelve hun-
                dred injuries, approximately thir-
                teen hundred arrests, and more
                than $10 million in property dam-
                age.

Source: <u>Newark Evening News</u>, July 16, 1967.

    The death toll in Newark's continuing rioting rose
to at least 20 early today as snipers continued a deadly
harassment from roof-tops and windows.
    Snipers fired at Fourth Precinct Police headquarters,
at a police helicopter, at National Guardsmen protecting
looted stores and at firehouses. Two firemen were
wounded.
    Seven new deaths were reported as the rioting con-
tinued. A detective resting at home from riot duty died
of a heart attack.
    More than 1,500 persons were treated for riot in-
juries at five of the city hospitals. As of last night,
more than 1,200 persons had been arrested.
    As the rampaging continued, National Guardsmen hast-
ily erected barbed wire in hard-hit streets near the
Irvington town line. At the Columbus Homes on Eleventh
Avenue, residents threw bottles at firemen extinguishing
a small fire in a store.

White Gangs Roam

    On Bloomfield Avenue near Mt. Prospect Avenue, po-
lice were rushed in to disperse gangs of white youths
roaming the area.
    At Chestnut and Orchard streets, only three blocks
from Newark City Hall, police came under heavy fire.
    Violence struck for the first time in the city's
predominantly-white Vailsburg area. At South Orange and
West End avenues, a group of youths began stoning cars.
Police also met resistance farther up at Brookdale Avenue.
    Police who rushed to the Columbus Homes on reports
of a sniper began shooting at men perched on the roofs
of the project, only to find they were exchanging fire
with National Guardsmen.
    Police stopped and searched all out-of-state cars
coming into the city from the New Jersey Turnpike.
    Although the riots were still centered in the Cen-
tral Ward, isolated cases of damage cropped up in other
areas of the city. Neighboring Irvington declared a

10 p.m. to 6 a.m. curfew, the same as that of Newark.

Patrolmen Targets

Shooting erupted shortly after 6 last night in front
of the Fourth Precinct police headquarters as a group of
patrolmen were leaving the building. The gunfire came
from the Hayes Homes opposite the precinct.

A police helicopter was summoned to flush out the
sniper. As the craft hovered over the housing projects,
he started shooting at it. The craft quickly spun around
and left before it was hit. Ground fire from police
finally forced the sniper to flee.

At the corner of Broad and Oriental streets, there
were persistent reports of shooting. Police shotgun
squads were sent to the area along with 100 National
Guardsmen. The Guardsmen were fired on, but they
couldn't locate any gunman.

Snipers also fired sporadically on National Guardsmen guarding looted and battered stores in Springfield
Avenue and Bergen Street.

The firehouse of Engine Co. 6 at Springfield Avenue and Hunterdon Street was placed out of service at
6:30 p.m. as shots were repeatedly fired at it. The
Fire house is a block away from the Hayes Homes.

Police HQ Barricaded

Franklin Street--where police headquarters is lo-
cated--was blocked off to all traffic. Barricades were
placed at Broad and Mulberry Streets leading to the
headquarters building.

In an effort to quiet the trouble-torn city, a volunteer group of Negro and white leaders entered the cordoned-off Central Ward to persuade residents to maintain
order.

Gov. Hughes ordered the state of emergency to remain in effect on the city through today. He said the
condition will be reviewed tomorrow morning.

As groups gathered in trouble spots, National
Guardsmen tried to disperse them. The groups, however,
reformed on another section of the street.

Groups continued to taunt police and guardsmen who
were the target of bottle barrages.

The restrictions imposed upon the city for another
24 hours by Gov. Hughes include a 10 p.m. curfew for vehicles and an 11 p.m. curfew for individuals; a ban on
all sales of liquor, and restricted travel through the
Central Ward.

Col. David B. Kelly, commandant of the New Jersey
State Police, ordered Springfield and South Orange avenues sealed off yesterday. State and local police along
with National Guardsmen quickly set up barricades at

all entrances to the main thoroughfares.

Only emergency vehicles and residents of the area were allowed in. Even the press was barred from the streets. Police carefully searched every vehicle entering the cordoned-off area.

Joseph Lordi, director of the Division of Alcoholic Beverage Control, ordered all Newark taverns and liquor stores closed until tomorrow when a decision will be made on their re-opening.

The second Newark policeman to die was Detective Fred Keller of 161 Norman Road, assigned to the Bureau of Special Assignments. He died at 12:10 a.m. yesterday. Keller had worked from 7 a.m. to 5 p.m., and was home resting when he was stricken with a heart attack. Keller had been with the force for 37 years.

Friday night Detective Fred Toto, 34, was killed by sniper bullets.

Damage was estimated in the millions of dollars.

As the tense situation continued, police became fearful that outside groups would converge on the heated city.

FBI Report

The Federal Bureau of Investigation office in Buffalo, N.Y., alerted Newark police yesterday that "20 or 30 carloads" of Negro youths were seen heading from Detroit to Newark.

In yesterday's looting, perhaps the hardest hit was the Hayes Drugstore in 264 15th Ave., that had survived three days of riots. Looters smashed large plate glass windows, entered the building and made off with more than $20,000 worth of drugs, including a large quantity of narcotics.

Detectives rounded up several suspects within an hour and recovered most of the drugs.

The Garden State Parkway closed exits 144 and 145 in both directions at noon yesterday on orders from Col. Kelly. The interchanges will remain closed until further notice, a spokesman said. Interchange 145 is located in Irvington and leads to South Orange Avenue, a main Newark traffic artery. Interchange 144 is located in East Orange and leads to Central Avenue, another heavily trafficked Newark approach road.

In the downtown business district, about a mile away from the riot area, most stores were closed for the day. Ohrbach's and Bamberger's, two of the city's largest department stores were among the closed. S. Klein's was open briefly then closed. Other shops boarded their windows with large plywood panels.

Everywhere in the city one could see National Guardsmen. They patrolled in front of stores, rode jeeps armed with machine guns and drove through in armored personnel carriers.

To patrol the area, it was divided into seven zones by National Guardsmen and State Police. The affected area is bounded by the Irvington-Newark line starting at South Orange Avenue and extending to Keer Avenue, to Elizabeth Avenue, to Clinton Avenue, to Washington Street, and along Washington Street. The area continues to Central Avenue, up Central Avenue to N. 12th Street and back to South Orange Avenue.

"Soul" Sign

Everywhere in the area could be seen the word "soul," a sort of password which means that a business or house is owned by a Negro. Most places with the word written on them were left unharmed.

But once the expression became known, even white businessmen painted it on their windows. One business-man, who asked that his name and address not be given, said: "What else can I do. If they don't get me tonight, they'll come around tomorrow. I can't think of anything else to do."

Even mail delivery was affected by the riots. All mail directed to Newark is being diverted to Philadelphia for the weekend. Postmaster Joseph J. Bennucci said there would be no deliveries of any type of mail or pick-ups and processing today.

THE GOVERNOR'S COMMISSION ON CIVIL DISORDER
-- 1968

> The section entitled "Findings"
> from the report of Governor Richard
> J. Hughes' commission to study the
> 1967 Newark riot, published on Feb-
> ruary 10, 1968, follows.

Source: Report for Action, Governor's Select Commission
on Civil Disorder, State of New Jersey, Trenton, 1968,
pp. 143-144.

1. The Newark City Administration did not adequately
realize the bitterness in important sectors of the Negro
community over the Administration's policies and conduct
in the medical school and Parker-Callaghan controversies.
The Administration did not seem to understand that political support by large numbers of Negroes in past municipal elections was not a guarantee against disaffection
and disappointment over specific issues of direct and
deep interest to Negroes. This reflects a serious lack
of communication between established authority and the
black community, which is one of the prime ills of Newark.

2.   There was virtually a complete breakdown in the
relations between the police and the Negro community prior
to the disorders, and there is no evidence that there
has been any improvement since July. Distrust, resentment and bitterness were at a high level on both sides,
and there was no evidence of any significant improvement
in this vital area when the Commission ended its hearings
late in 1967.

3.   Pre-riot planning by the Newark Police Department was inadequate. The department did not have sufficient resources for riot control, and it had not prepared a plan of operations for coping with the possibili-
ty of large-scale disorders.

4.   Those who passed out leaflets and called for a
rally on the evening of Thursday, July 13, in front of
the Fourth Precinct, following the night of the Smith
arrest, showed poor judgment. In the light of the high
state of tension in the community, a rally was far more
likely to lead to disorder than to nonviolent protest.

5.   The Administration of the City of Newark was
too hesitant to request State Police assistance, despite
the views of high officers in the Newark Police Department that such aid was needed. Had aid been requested
earlier, the rioting might have been contained more
quickly and effectively.

6.   Once assistance was requested, the State respond-
ed promptly and with adequate forces. However, due to

the absence of an adequate plan for the control of disorders setting forth the command structure among the various law enforcement elements, delays and other problems arose that inhibited the effectiveness of the overall effort.

7. The inability of the various police forces to broadcast over one another's radio frequencies created major communications problems. The absence of a single radio communications channel for all police forces hampered the performance of all riot-control elements.

8. The amount of ammunition expended by police forces was out of all proportion to the mission assigned to them. All police forces lacked an adequate system of ammunition control. No proper procedures had been established for dispensing and accounting for the expenditure of ammunition. The use of personal weapons by members of the Newark Police Department created special problems in this area and should be condemned.

9. The technique of employing heavy return fire at suspected sniper locations proved tragic and costly.

10. The heavy firing by police elements against suspected snipers makes it difficult to determine the extensiveness of sniping. There may have been some organized sniping activity once the riot had reached its Friday peak.

11. There is evidence of prejudice against Negroes during the riot on the part of various police and National Guard elements. This resulted in the use of excessive and unjustified force and other abuses against Negro citizens.

12. The damage caused within a few hours early Sunday morning, July 16, to a large number of stores marked with "Soul" signs to depict non-white ownership and located in a limited area reflects a pattern of police action for which there is no possible justification. Testimony strongly suggests that State Police elements were mainly responsible with some participation by National Guardsmen. These raids resulted in personal suffering and economic damage to innocent small businessmen and property owners who have a stake in law and order and who had not participated in any unlawful act. It embittered the Negro community as a whole at a time when the disorders had begun to ebb.

13. The evidence presented to the Commission does not support the thesis of a conspiracy or plan to initiate the Newark riot.

PRESSURE BY PUERTO RICANS TO IMPROVE
THEIR LOT -- 1969

> In February 1969 residents of Puer-
> to Rican background demanded of the
> city council that steps be taken to
> improve their living conditions.

Source: Newark Evening News, February 6, 1969.

About 200 persons, including about 40 "Puerto Rican
hippies" literally stormed the City Council meeting last
night demanding that the city government take steps to
improve the lot of the 50,000 /sic/ Puerto Ricans in
Newark.

Armed with a three-page typewritten list of "recommendations," which also included several complaints,
the Puerto Ricans demanded better living conditions,
freedom from harassment by police, more city jobs and
appointment of a Puerto Rican magistrate.

They received a promise of a meeting next week with
the council, Mayor Hugh J. Addonizio and members of the
United Community Corporation, the city's antipoverty a-
gency after a short, but heated dialogue with the council members.

Discrimination Charged

Speaking theough as many as three spokesmen, some-
times all at once, the Puerto Ricans charged that both
business and government discriminate against them prin-
cipally because of their difficulty with the English
language.

Apparently thinking they would have an audience with
the mayor last night, they expressed their unhappiness
that Addonizio "did not have the courtesy to make the
appointment."

The group appeared in the council chambers following
several hours of picketing in front of City Hall to dem-
onstrate their demands.

The Puerto Ricans listed in their "recommendations"
a series of complaints including:

Complaints Listed

Thousands of Puerto Ricans in Newark live in substandard houses, infested with rats and other vermin;
jobs, both in private industry and in government are de-
nied Puerto Ricans, and even when they are hired, they
are paid wages lower than those paid to English-speaking
workers doing the same jobs; welfare payments are too low
to properly feed and clothe their families; police often

accost Puerto Ricans for no reason, and Puerto Ricans are often jailed for long periods without communication with the outside world, simply because they do not understand or speak English and the police do not speak Spanish.

Rafael Lozada, one of the several spokesmen, noted that the Puerto Rican community "is uniting to get solutions to these wrongs." It was he who stated that "even the Puerto Rican hippies are with us," pointing to the back of the chamber, where about 40 young people, dressed in spangled denim jackets sat quietly and apparently interested in the proceedings.

He also told the council: "There are 200 of us who are willing to walk for hours outside in 20-degree weather to get what we deserve. Summer is coming, and you know what that means."

Imperiale Response

Councilman-At-Large Anthony Imperiale took exception to the remark about the summer, calling it a "veiled threat." Imperiale said that "nobody is going to riot in the summer in Newark. We've had enough of that."

Victor Lopez, another spokesman, who said he has lived in Newark since he was one year old, said, "We're not asking for anything except what we deserve."

Lopez and Imperiale huddled briefly after the meeting to discuss the scheduled meeting. They said later that they would make arrangements today.

To eliminate the unsanitary living conditions, the group suggested that the city appoint several Puerto Ricans to key positions in the Health Department. Puerto Ricans in the Welfare Department would solve some of the problems in that area, also, they said.

They noted that "while almost all city departments say, and do try to serve the Puerto Rican community, they are handicapped in giving real service becayse of the language and ethnic barrier." More Spanish-speaking persons in every department would solve that problem, they said.

They urged "proper legal services" be set up to serve the Puerto Ricans, to preclude arrests and incarcerations of persons who cannot understand what is going on.

They urged also that Spanish-speaking personnel be stationed in all police precincts, and courts, and criticized the fact that while police "Community Relations Offices have been set up, none has a Puerto Rican director."

THE CHERRY BLOSSOM FESTIVAL'S
SEVENTY-FIFTH ANNIVERSARY -- 1970

On April 19, 1970, the city observed
the seventy-fifth annual Cherry Blossom Festival in Branch Brook Park.

Source: Newark Star-Ledger, April 12, 1970.

Original Japanese music and dancing will highlight
the 75th Anniversary Cherry Blossom Festival in Branch
Brook Park, Newark, next Sunday.

The program will begin at 1:30 p.m. in the Belleville extension of the park, north of Heller Parkway.

A brief ceremony commemorating the founding of the
park system 75 years ago -- making it the oldest county
park in the United States -- will be presided over by
Hiroshi Uchida, Japanese Consul at New York.
* * *
The program is being presented in cooperation with
the Japanese American Association of New York, William
R. Harris, chairman of the anniversary committee.

No reservations or tickets are needed to attend,
Harris said. "Everyone is cordially invited to bring
their families and enjoy this short-run spring extrava-
ganza of cherry blossoms."

The Japanese American Association considers the display of cherry blossoms at Branch Brook the largest and
most unique in the world. Nearly 400 Japanese-Americans
are expected to attend, some wearing traditional Japanese
attire.

Yoshi Imai, an executive of Walston & Co., Newark,
is co-chairman of the outing for the Association.
* * *
There are 2,200 ornamental cherry trees and about
four different species in what was, in 1895, swampland.
The first trees were provided by the Felix Fuld family
of Newark during the late 1920s.

The park today contains 500 acres of trees, shrubs
and a beautiful lawn-bordered lake.

The object of the 75th anniversary Committee in
planning such events as the Cherry Blossom Festival is to
focus more public interest and attention on the park system's accomplishments over the last 75 years so that support may be gained for future park development in the
county.

Entertainment at the festival will be provided by
top members of Miss Miyoko Wantanabe's well-known Japanese dancing group, which has performed for a number of
dignitaries, including Prince and Princess Mikasa at the
World's Fair,....

THE INAUGURATION OF MAYOR GIBSON -- 1970

> On July 1, 1970, Kenneth A. Gibson
> was inaugurated as the first black
> mayor of Newark.

Source: <u>Newark Star Ledger</u>, July 2, 1970.

"I want to restore our city's good name. I want to
make it a good place to live, work and worship."

Speaking to a crowd of more than 8,000 and pledging
to unite the city, Kenneth A. Gibson yesterday became the
first black mayor of Newark. -- Cries of "Right on!" came
frequently from the throng as Gibson, with dignitaries
from across the country listening to his words, pledged
his administration to work hard to reverse the deteriora-
tion of city life, the restoration of morale at City Hall
and the improvement of city services and education.

Following his swearing-in on a platform erected over
the steps of City Hall, Gibson, wearing a gray, pin-
striped suit, dark blue tie and blue shirt, told the
crowd:

"First, I must pay tribute to those who made our
victory possible. They come from all neighborhoods in
the city. They are young and old; they are black, brown
and white -- they represent a wide spectrum of the cultural
and nationality groups which make up Newark. They had
faith in me and in our cause. I hope to fulfill that
faith by bringing Newark onto a new track in the opening
years of the 1970s."

Behind Gibson on the rostrum fluttered the American
flag and the flags of New Jersey and the City of Newark.

Seated on the platform as he spoke were: Gov. William
T. Cahill; Edmund Hume, state commissioner of community
affairs; Dr. Robert Cowan, state commissioner of health;
the Rev. Ralph David Abernathy, successor to Dr. Martin
Luther King Jr. as head of the Southern Christian Leadership Conference; Herman Badillo of New York City, a can-
didate trying to become the first Puerto Rican elected
to Congress; black Mayors William S. Hart Jr. of East
Orange and Matthew Carter of Montclair; Manhattan Borough President Percy Sutton; and Gustave Henningburg,
president of the Greater Newark Urban Coalition.

Absent from the inauguration was former Mayor Hugh
J. Addonizio, who was in Trenton at his trial on extor-
tion-conspiracy and income tax evasion charges.

. . .

To bring "Newark onto a new track in the opening
years of the 1970s," would require, said Gibson, "hard
work and civic pride. We also need as much help from
private business, public agencies and all levels of government as we can get."

Gibson outline plans for sprucing up the city's
neighborhood downtown shopping areas. A rolling shout
of approval greeted his proposal for "better policing."
He singled out for special consideration industrial
location in the city's Meadowlands areas and expansion
of mass transportation facilities.
"The unfinished highway projects would devastate
portions of our city like hurricanes and for which hun-
dreds of people have been displaced, must be completed
as swiftly as possible. These are just a few of the
items relating to the economy that need attention," he
said.
Gibson vowed also to eliminate waste of manpower
and funds, "especially in costly over-construction and
substandard work by contractions."
Gibson said he expected the Board of Education,
"whose full membership I will have appointed by the end
of three years," to become the leading force for improving
the city's school system.
"The schools today," he said, "are instruments of
social progress or of backsliding. For us in Newark, they
must be the means of training a generation of young people to enter productive work."
The new mayor also urged cooperation from institutions of higher learning in the city.
"I hope the leaders of these growing institutions
will fight for our city," he said. "They can do this
by requesting of the State Board of Higher Education
that payments in lieu of taxes be made to Newark for the
tax-free land they occupy and for the services we will-
ingly provide.
"They can also do this by viewing with a sympathetic
eye. . . the rising interest of our high school graduates
in advanced education."
Gibson repeated his pledge not to "make widespread
or vindictive purges of city employes." He knew, he said,
there were many skilled and dedicated employes in every
department.
"Unfortunately," he continued, "the visible crisis
through which our city has passed in the recent decade
has gravely affected morale. . .relfected in a decline
in the quality of many services and in plant and equipment."
Inviting all city employes "to join with me," he said
every one in the city will expect now "a full day's work
for a day's pay."
Gibson said he was not asking for a grace period even
though "Newark did not reach its present condition overnight. And it will not become the city we want it to become, overnight, either." But, he said, "we are beginning a drive to reverse a trend...."

BIBLIOGRAPHY

The number of primary sources and secondary works relating to the long and varied history of Newark, New Jersey, is considerable. There are two main depositories of materials: the Archives of Newark City Hall and the New Jersey Reference Division of the Newark Public Library. The latter makes available to users a well-or dered guide to its extensive collection. The New Jersey Historical Society in Newark and the New Jersey State Library in Trenton also hold important items on Newark.

UNPUBLISHED CITY DOCUMENTS

Minutes of the Meetings of the Common Council, 1836-1917.

PRINTED CITY DOCUMENTS

Annual Messages of the Mayor.

Annual Reports of the Board of Education.

Annual Reports of the Board of Fire Commissioners.

Annual Reports of the Board of Health.

Annual Reports of the Chief of Police.

Annual Reports of the City Clerk.

Annual Reports of the City Treasurer.

Annual Reports of the Department of Health and Welfare.

Annual Reports of the Department of Parks and Public Property.

Annual Reports of the Department of Public Works.

Annual Reports of the Department of Revenue and Finance.

Annual Reports of the Director of Public Safety.

Manuals of the Board of Commissioners.

Manuals of the Common Council.

Minutes of the Meetings of the Board of Commissioners, 1918-1954.

Minutes of the Meetings of the City Council, 1954-to date,

Records of the Town of Newark, New Jersey, From Its
     Settlement in 1666, To Its Incorporation As a
     City in 1836. Newark:The New Jersey Historical
     Society, 1864.

Reports of the Newark Central Planning Board.

Reports of the Newark Housing Authority.

Reports of the Newark Human Rights Commission.

Reports of the Newark Office of Economic Development.

                PRINTED STATE DOCUMENTS

Report for Action, Governor's Select Commission on Civil
     Disorder, State of New Jersey. Trenton, 1968.

                NON-GOVERNMENT REPORTS

Annual Reports of the Chamber of Commerce of the City of
     Newark.

Holden. Edgar. Mortality and Sanitary Records of Newark,
     N.J., 1859-1879: A Report Presented to the President
     and Director of the Mutual Benefit Life Insurance
     Company. Newark, 1880.

Yearbooks of the Newark Board of Trade.

                    DIRECTORIES

Newark Business Directory, 1908-41.

Newark City Directory, 1835-1965.

                    NEWSPAPERS

Evening Press, 1890-91.

The Jacksonian, 1847-57.

New Jersey Eagle, 1820-47.

New Jersey Freie Zeitung, 1857-to date.

New Jersey Life Boat, 1853-54.

Newark Daily Advertiser, 1832-1907.

Newark Daily Courier, 1876-77.

Newark Daily Eagle, 1853-57.

Newark Daily Journal, 1862-94.

Newark Daily Mercury, 1848-63.

Newark Eagle, 1915-16.

Newark Evening Courier, 1866-76.

Newark Evening Journal, 1857-62.

Newark Evening Ledger, 1916-19.

Newark Evening News, 1890-1972.

Newark Evening Star, 1907-15.

Newark Gazette, 1797-1804.

Newark Inquirer, 1834-35.

Newark Ledger, 1916-39.

Newark Monitor, 1829-32.

Newark Morning Eagle, 1847-53.

Newark Morning Ledger, 1916-19.

Newark Morning Press, 1889-90.

Newark Morning Register, 1869-86.

Newark Morning Star and Newark Advertiser, 1906-15.

Newark Press Register, 1889-90.

Newark Star Eagle, 1916-39.

Newark Star-Ledger, 1939 - to date.

Newark Sunday News, 1946-72.

Newark Weekly Journal, 1857-66.

People's Paper, 1871.

Rosebud, 1840-41.

Sentinel of Freedom, 1796-1895.

Sunday Call, 1872-1946.

Sunday Standard, 1889-96.

Wood's Newark Gazette, 1791-97.

BOOKS

Atkinson, Joseph. The History of Newark, New Jersey.
     Newark: William B. Guild, 1878.

Benson, Ann H. Newark-In-Print. Newark: The Public Li-
     brary, 1931.

Biographical and Genealogical History of the City of
     Newark and Essex County, New Jersey. vol. I. New
     York: The Lewis Publishing Company, 1898.

Cunningham, John T. Newark. Newark: The New Jersey
     Historical Society, 1966.

Folsom, Joseph Fulford. The Municipalities of Essex
     County, New Jersey, 1666-1924, vols. I and II.
     New York: Lewis Historical Publishing Company, Inc.,
     1925.

Hayden, Tom. Rebellion in Newark. New York: Vintage
     Books, 1967.

Historic Newark. Boston: Walton Advertising & Printing
     Company, 1916.

Kingdon, Frank. John Cotton Dana. Newark: The Public
     Library and Museum, 1940.

Newark, The Metropolis of New Jersey, At the Dawn of the
     Twentieth Century. The Progress of One Hundred
     Years. Newark: Progress Publishing Co., 1901.

Pierson, David Lawrence. Narratives of Newark (In New
     Jersey) From the Days of Its Founding, 1666-1916.
     Newark: Pierson Publishing Co., 1917.

Rankin, Edward S. Indian Trails and City Streets. Mont-
     clair, N.J.: Montclair Globe Press, 1927.

----------------. Running Brooks and Other Sketches of
     Early Newark. Somerville, N.J.: Unionist-Gazette,
     1930.

Rankin, John L. Newark Charter Studies. Newark, 1910.

Shaw, William H. History of Essex and Hudson Counties,
     New Jersey. vol. I. Philadelphia: Evarts & Peck,

1884.

Urquhart, Frank J. A History of the City of Newark, New
     Jersey. 3 vols. New York: The Lewis Historical
     Publishing Co., 1913.

----------------. A Short History of Newark. Newark:
     Baker Printing Company, 1908.

----------------. A Short History of Newark. Newark:
     Baker Printing Company, 1953.

Van Deusen, Helen Peters Dodd. The Newark of Former
     Days and the Newark of To Day. Newark: The Free
     Public Library, 1907.

                          PAMPHLETS

Bannwart, Carl. History of Military Park and a Sketch of
     the Monument. Newark: The Public Library, 1926.

Board of Trade. Newark--A City of Manufacturers: Report
     for 1896. Newark, 1895.

Doremus, Henry M. Growth of Newark. Newark, 1903.

First Baptist Peddie Memorial Church of Newark, N.J.
     Program of Centennial Observance, June Second to
     June Ninth. Newark, 1901.

Handbook and Guide for the City of Newark, 1872. New-
     ark, 1872.

History of the Police Department of Newark, N.J. Newark,
     1893.

Leary, Peter J. Newark, N.J., Illustrated: A Souvenir
     of the City and Its Numerous Industries. Newark,
     1893.

Lewin, William. Newark, 1666-1776-1926. Newark: The
     Public Library, 1926.

MacDougall, A. W. (ed.). The Philanthropies of Newark,
     New Jersey. n.p., 1916.

Newark and Its Businessmen. Newark, 1891.

Newark, the Metropolis of New Jersey, At the Dawn of the
     Twentieth Century. The Progress of One Hundred
     Years. Newark: Progress Publishing Co., 1901.

The Newark Museum: A Chronicle of the Founding Years,
    1909-1934. Newark, n.d.

Newark's Last Fifteen Years, 1904-1919. Newark, 1919.

Price, Willard D. The Ironbound District: A Study of a
    District in Newark, N. J. Newark: The Neighborhood
    House, 1912.

Proceedings Commemorative of the Settlement of Newark,
    N. J., on the 200th Anniversary, May 17, 1866.
    Newark: The New Jersey Historical Society, 1866.

Report and Catalogue of the First Exhibition of Newark
    Industries, 1872. Newark, 1882.

Seth Boyden of Newark. Newark: The Public Library, 1925.

Stearns, Jonathan French. Historical Discourses Relating
    to the First Presbyterian Church in Newark. New-
    ark, 1853.

Thowless, Herbert L. Historical Sketch of the City of
    Newark, N. J. Newark, 1903.

Urquhart, Frank J., Newark: The Story of Its Early Days.
    Newark, 1904.

Winser, Henry Jacob (ed.). Metropolis of New Jersey:
    Newark, Her Past Growth and Future Development.
    Newark, 1896.

--------------------. Trinity Church, Newark. Celebra-
    tion of the One Hundred and Fiftieth Anniversary.
    Newark, 1896.

                          SERIALS

Newark! Newark: The Chamber of Commerce, 1967-to date.

Newark Commerce. Newark: The Chamber of Commerce,
    1957-66.

The Newarker. Newark: The Free Public Library, 1911-16.

The Newarker. Newark: The Chamber of Commerce, 1922-28.

The Newarker. Newark: The Junior Chamber of Commerce,
    1948-57.

ARTICLES

Allen, Charles R. "Newark Wary of Heretic Hunters,"
    Nation, CLXXXI (July 16, 1955), inside cover.

"All-Year Schools; Experiment Made in Newark, New Jer-
    sey," Elementary School Journal, XVI (June 1916),
    516-20.

Alsop, Stewart. "American Sickness," Saturday Evening
    Post, CCXLI (July 13, 1968), 6.

Anderson, Jervis. "Voices of Newark; Central Ward Con-
    ditions," Commentary, XLIV (October 1967), 85-90.

"Another Big City Elects a Negro Mayor," U.S. News and
    World Report, LXVIII (June 29, 1970), 46.

"Autopsy in Newark," Newsweek, LXXI (February 19, 1968),
    28.

Baker, Benjamin. "Newark Gets a Modern City Charter,"
    The American City, LXIX (February 1954), 106-07.

Bannwart, Carl. "Newark Pioneers Steadily in Tree Care,"
    The American City, XLIII (August 1930), 140-41.

Barclay, Dorothy. "Their Museum Comes to Life," New
    York Times Magazine, (October 26, 1952), 42.

Bartholomew, Harland. "Publicity and the City Plan,"
    The American City, XI (November 1914), 380-82.

Bates, Frank G. "Municipal Charter Revision: Newark,"
    American Political Science Review, V (August 1911),
    438-40.

"Black Mayors," Newsweek, LXXVI (August 3, 1970), 21-22.

"Block Playgrounds in Newark," Playground, XVIII (De-
    cember 1924), 547.

Campbell, Christie. "It Fits In! Air Force ROTC,"
    Flying, LV (December 1954), 26-27.

Caplan, Nathan S. and Paige, Jeffrey M. "Study of Ghetto
    Rioters," Scientific American, CCIX (August 1968),
    15-21.

Caprio, Ralph G. and Crann, Frank. "Resourceful Street
    Maintenance," The American City, LXXVIII (April
    1963), 96-97.

Carter, Luther J.   "Newark: Negroes Demand and Get Voice
      in Medical School Plans; New Jersey College of Medi-
      cine and Dentistry," Science, CLX (April 19, 1968),
      290-92.

"Child Guidance in Newark," School and Society, XXIII
      (April 17, 1926), 489-90.

"City: Problems of a Prototype," Time, XCIII (March 21,
      1969), 21.

"City's Anniversary," Outlook, CXIII (July 12, 1916), 609.

"Closing Hurt Newark, PNYA Head Says," Aviation Week,
      LVI (May 5, 1952), 18.

Coates, Robert M.   "The Art Galleries," New Yorker,
      XXXIII (April 20, 1957), 102-05.

Colbert, Stanley L. "$50 Million Face-Lifting at Newark,"
      Aviation Week, XLVIII (May 3, 1948), 40.

Cook, Fred J.   "It's Our City, Don't Destroy It," New
      York Times Magazine, (June 30, 1968), 10-11.

Cooper, Samuel E.   "Newark Wary of Heretic Hunters; Re-
      ply," Nation, CLXXXI (December 3, 1955), inside
      cover.

Corson, David B.   "Some Ideals and Accomplishments of
      the Newark School System," National Education
      Association. Proceedings and Addresses, (1921),
      707-13.

Craster, Charles V.   "Slum Clearance; Newark Plan,"
      American Journal of Public Health and Nation's
      Health, XXXIV (September 1944), 935-40.

Costello, James W.   "Newark, N. J., Contracts for Gar-
      bage Disposal," The American City, XXI (October
      1919), 314.

"Courses in Radio Appreciation; Student Themes from Bar-
      ringer High School," Education, LXII (March 1942),
      390-96.

"Crackdown in New Jersey," Time, XCIV (December 19, 1969),
      17.

Cunningham, John T.   "To Walk a Different Way; Weequahic
      and Branch Brook Parks," Parks & Recreation, V (Jan-
      uary 1970), 26-28.

Dana, John Cotton. "Museum Of, For and By Newark,"
    Survey, LV (March 1, 1926), 613-17.

----------------. "Preparing for Newark's Two-Hundred-
    and-Fiftieth Birthday," The American City, XIII
    (December 1916), 531-33.

----------------. "Relations of the Library to the
    City," The American City, VII (October 1912), 314-
    17.

"Dana: Prophet of Newark," Newsweek, XXIV (December 4,
    1944), 106.

Deschin, Jacob. "Newark's Branch Libraries in Depart-
    ment Stores," The Library Journal, LVII (March 15,
    1932), 273-74.

"Diphtheria Immunization in Newark," American Journal of
    Public Health and Nation's Health, XXVI (October
    1936), 1007.

Ditmars, I. E. "The Cathedral of the Sacred Heart, New-
    ark, New Jersey," Architectural Record, LIX (June
    1926), 501-11.

Doremus, Goline. "Newark Develops a New Dump-Truck Body
    for Waste Collection," The American City, XL (April
    1929), 97.

"Double Jeopardy in Newark," Time, XCV (June 15, 1970),
    20.

Duffy, Michael P. "Newark Fire Department: Man-Power,
    Methods and Equipment," The American City, LI
    (November 1936), 50-52.

Dwight, H. G. "Newark Bay; Poem," Atlantic Monthly,
    CXVIII (September 1916), 338-40.

Evenson, John. "'Thinking Black' in Newark," Christi-
    anity Today, XIII (November 22, 1968), 41.

Farrand, Wilson, and O'Shea, M. V. "Report: The All-
    Year Schools in Newark," School and Society, XXIII
    (April 10, 1926), 462-69.

"Fear Is a Vacant Store," Business Week, (April 13,
    1968), 33.

"Fire Last Time," Senior Scholastic, XCII (February 29,
    1968), 20-21.

"Fire-Traps Found in Newark," Charities, X (June 13, 1903), 588-91.

Fishback, Howard G. "Commission Government Has Not Redeemed Newark," The Annals of the American Academy of Political and Social Science, CXCIX (September 1938), 71-77.

Francisco, Ellsworth. "Newark, N. J., Makes Rapid Progress in Improving Street Lighting," The American City, XXXIX (July 1928), 96-98.

"Fresh Air in Newark; K. Gibson Takes Over as Mayor," Life, LXIX (July 4, 1970), 42-43.

Fried, Antoinette. "Work Camp Programs for Potential Delinquents," The Annals of the American Academy of Political and Social Science, CCCXXII (March 1959), 38-46.

"From Tin-Cans to Peas 'n' Beans," Independent and Weekly Review, XCIX (July 12, 1919), 43-45.

Garrison, Glenn. "Newark Wins Back Airline Business," Aviation Week, LXV (July 16, 1956), 41-43.

"Garyized Schools in Newark," Manual Training and Vocational Education, XIX (January 1918), 175-76.

"Gas and Electric Light Service," Annals of the American Academy of Political and Social Science, XXVII (January 1906), 217-18.

Gasser, Henry. "Henry Gasser's Paintings of Newark," American Artist, XXX (November 1966), 48-53.

Gates, Marguerite L. "Shade Tree Commission Landscapes Library Grounds," The American City, LV (January 1940), 87.

"Gibson's Victory," New Yorker, XLVI (June 27, 1970), 28-29.

Giles, Nell. "Teen-Age Trouble," Ladies Home Journal, LX (November 1943), 24-25.

Gillen, Charles P. "Army Food Sales By the City of Newark," The American City, XXI (October 1919), 347-48.

Gilliams, E. Leslie. "A Library for Business Men," System, XXIV (August 1913), 188-90.

Goldberger, Paul. "Tony Imperiale Stands Vigilant for

Law and Order," New York Times Magazine, (September 29, 1968), 30.

Goldmann, Robert. "Newark Riot Report's Missing Ingredient; Reply," New Republic, CLVIII (March 16, 1968), 35.

"Griffith Foundation Lists Newark Series," Musical America, LXXIV (December 15, 1954), 16.

Gross, Kenneth G. "A Cold Night in July," Esquire, LXIX (February 1968), 134.

Haddon, Rawson W. "Modern American Schoolhouses," Architectural Record, XXXVI (September 1914), 244-63.

Hart, Charles. "The Reformed Protestant Dutch Church in Newark," Proceedings of the New Jersey Historical Society, new series, II (July 1917), 7-19.

"Heirs to Disaster; Newark's Mayoralty Race," Newsweek, LXXV (May 25, 1970), 63.

Hennings, Alice B. ". . . a Teacher Answers the Challenge," Ladies Home Journal, LXXIII (September 1956), 89.

Holzhauser, M. "Newark Museum's Summer Program for Young People," School Arts, XLV (May 1946), 300-01.

Hopkins, Mary Alden. "The Newark Factory Fire," McClure's Magazine, XXXVI (April 1911), 663-72.

"How Businessmen Pitched In To Save a City," Nation's Business, LVIII (December 1970), 44-48.

Howard, J. W. "Cost of Pavement Repairs in Newark, N. J." The American City, XXVIII (April 1923), 338.

Hughes, Richard J. "The Lessons of New Jersey's Race Riots; Interview," U.S. News & World Report, LXIII (July 31, 1967), 32-36.

Hunt, William S. "Why a Newark, Anyhow?" Proceedings of the New Jersey Historical Society, LIV (July 1936), 224-28.

"Illuminating the Facade of a County Court House," The American City, XXVII (October 1922), 369-71.

"Is Newark Penny-Wise and Pound-Foolish?" Survey, XXXVI (May 13, 1916), 173-74.

"John Cotton Dana and the Newark Museum," Magazine of
    Art, XXXVIII (November 1944), 268-70.

Kaufman, George S.   "Does Newark Have to Be Where It Is?"
    New Yorker, XXIX (September 19, 1953), 33.

Keenan, John B.   "Catching Up on Traffic Control," The
    American City, LXI (November 1946), 114-15.

--------------.   "Newark's 962 Parking Meters Collecting
    $6,000 Per Month," The American City, LVIII (Feb-
    ruary 1943), 60.

Kirk, Marguerite.   "Library Service for Elementary
    Schools in Newark, New Jersey," The Library Journal,
    LIX (September 15, 1934), 687-89.

Kirwan, J. D.   "One Man's Newark," National Review, XIX
    (August 8, 1967), 847.

Kuh, Katharine.   "Art Over the Counter," Saturday Review,
    XLIX (December 31, 1966), 38-39.

Lamb, Martha J.   "Newark," Harper's New Monthly Magazine,
    LIII (October 1876), 660-78.

Lerrigo, Ruth A.   "From Alms to Welfare; Newark Reaches
    a New Goal," The Survey, LXIX (April 1933), 149-50.

"Let Us Enjoy Our Victory; Black Victory, White Reac-
    tions," Newsweek, LXXV (June 29, 1970), 16-19.

Lewis, Frederick.   "American Cities; Travelchart," Wo-
    man's Home Companion, LV (February 1928), 124-25.

"Low-Cost Housing in Newark," Survey, LXV (January 15,
    1931), 444.

McAndrew, William.   "Making Newark Notorious," Educational
    Review, LXXIII (May 1927), 234-36.

Macdougall, R. B.   "Teenagers on Television; Junior Town
    Meeting," Journal of the National Educational Asso-
    ciation, XLI (May 1952), 284-85.

McKeon, Peter J.   "Fires, Factories and Prevention; the
    Newark Casualty--the New York Dangers," The Survey,
    XXV (January 7, 1911), 532-38.

Mangel, Charles.   "Violent Man Rises in Newark: T. Im-
    periale," Look, XXXIII (September 9, 1969), 62-67.

"Market Street Station; Views and Plan," Architectural

Record, LXXIX (March 1936), 199-205.

Mills, W. J. "West Point and Newark," _Delineator_, LXVI (August 1905), 257-59.

"More Useful Public Library," _World's Work_, XXV (March 1913), 504-05.

Moroze, Lewis M. "Newark: Lethal Indifference," _Nation_, CCV (August 14, 1967), 105-07.

Murphy, Vincent J. "Indexing Every Dollar Spent in the City," _The American City_, LIV (March 1939), 71.

"New Chance for Newark," _Christian Century_, LXXXVII (July 8, 1970), 837.

"New Jersey and the Newark Fire," _Survey_, XXVI (July 15, 1911), 575-78.

"New Jersey WPA Converts City Dump Into a Park," _The American City_, LII (December 1937), 83.

"New Mayor Tries for a New Newark," _Business Week_, (June 27, 1970), 36.

"New Pool Keeps City Cool," _The American City_, LXXXIV (December 1969), 36.

"New Terminal for Newark," _Flying_, LIII (October 1953), 41.

"New Times, Better Police," _The American City_, LXXVI (June 1961), 119.

"Newark Airport," _News-Week_, IX (February 6, 1937), 24-25.

"Newark Board Success: Local Mediation Group Averts Strikes," _Business Week_, (July 15, 1939), 43.

"Newark Board of Trade," _World's Work_, XVIII (June 1909), 654-55.

"Newark Boils Over," _Newsweek_, LXX (July 24, 1967), 21-22.

"Newark City Council Votes to Drop Library," _The Library Journal_, XCIV (March 15, 1969), 1081, 1083.

"Newark--the City of Industry," _Bulletin of the Pan-American Union_, XLVIII (May 1919), 504-16.

"Newark Employment Clinic," _Business Week_, (December 13, 1941), 78.

"Newark Gets Underground Parking Garage," _The American City_, LXXV (February 1960), 137.

"Newark Health Work Needs Reorganization," Survey,
    XXX (July 12, 1913), 495-96.

"Newark Library Economy Programs," The Library Journal,
    LVIII (May 1, 1933), 411.

"Newark Museum Purchases Paintings by State Artists,"
    Hobbies, LXIII (July 1958), 55.

"Newark Race Riot: Open Rebellion, Just Like Wartime,"
    U.S. News & World Report, LXIII (July 24, 1967), 6.

"Newark: Scarred, Scared, But Hopeful," Business Week,
    (July 29, 1967), 25.

"Newark Signs Up a Business Team," Business Week, (Au-
    gust 15, 1970), 23.

"Newark Stages Big Blackout in East's First Air Raid Re-
    hearsal," Life, X (June 9, 1941), 40-41.

"Newark Terminal Tries Innovations," Aviation Week, LIX
    (September 21, 1953), 70.

"Newark--the City of Industry," Bulletin of the Pan-
    American Union, XLVIII (May 1919), 504-16.

Nichols, Walter S. "Early Newark as a Puritan Theocracy
    in Colonial New Jersey," Proceedings of the New
    Jersey Historical Society, new series, V (October
    1920), 201-24.

"Notes and Comment: Actions of Police, State Troopers,
    and National Guardsmen," New Yorker, XLII (July 22,
    1967), 23-25.

Nunn, W. L. "Municipal Labor Boards of Toledo and New-
    ark," Monthly Labor Review, XLIX (November 1939),
    1045-49.

"One More Northern City Looks at Its Race Problem," U.S.
    News & World Report, XLIII (November 1, 1957), 65-67.

O'Neill, Frank. "Municipal Rescue Squads for Any Emer-
    gency," The American City, LIV (October 1939), 54-55.

"Opening of the Newark Museum," Libraries, XXXI (July
    1926), 364-66.

"Opera in Newark," Musician, XLVII (February 1942), 19.

O'Shea, John. "Newark Negroes Move Toward Power," At-
    lantic, CCXVI (November 1965), 90-92.

Pangburn, W. W. "Recreation in Newark," Journal of the
    National Education Association, XXII (December
    1933), 246-47.

Phillips, Harvey E. "Newark," Opera News, XXXIV (March
    7, 1970), 33.

Plotnik, Arthur. "Victory From the Jaws of Defeat: A
    Tribute to the Newark Public Library," Wilson Li-
    brary Bulletin, XLIII (April 1969), 740-45.

"Port Authority Seeks Permission to Open Newark Airport
    to Jet Traffic," Aviation Week & Space Technology,
    LXXIV (May 29, 1961), 34.

"Port Newark Terminal," The American City, XIV (April
    1916), 333-34.

"Poverty Plums: Anti-Poverty Operations," The Reporter,
    XXXII (March 11, 1965), 16.

"Progress & Poison: Medical School to Be Built in Cen-
    tral Ward on Terms Residents Welcome," Time, XCI
    (March 29, 1968), 25.

Rankin, Edward S. "The Purchase of Newark From the In-
    dians," Proceedings of the New Jersey Historical
    Society, new series, XIII (October 1927), 442-45.

Rankin, John L. "Newark Town Government from 1666-1833,"
    Proceedings of the New Jersey Historical Society,
    X (November 1915), 49-61.

Raymond, Thomas L. "Newark's Anniversary Celebration,"
    The American City, XIV (May 1916), 491-93.

"Real Tragedy of Newark," U.S. News & World Report,
    LXIII (July 31, 1967), 30-31.

"Reconstruction of the Lackawanna Tracks Through Newark,"
    Scientific American, XC (January 2, 1904), 10-13.

"Renaissance at Bamberger's," Publishers' Weekly, CLXXXIV
    (December 2, 1963), 24.

"Report of a Useful Public Library," School Review, XII
    (October 1904), 664-67.

Rhind, J. Massey. "Story of the Newark Copy of the
    Colleoni," Architectural Record, XLI (May 1917),
    475-78.

Rood, Henry. "Where Taxpayers Stand Treat," Harper's

Weekly, LIX (September 19, 1914), 281.

"Roseville Days--a View of Newark Boyhood in 1888 by One of the Boys," _Proceedings of the New Jersey Historical Society_, new series, XII (October 1927), 445-51.

Roth, Philip. "Reflections on the Death of a Library," _Wilson Library Bulletin_, XLIII (April 1969), 746-47.

"S. Klein's on the Move," _Newsweek_, XXXV (March 6, 1950), 60.

Sanfelici, Arthur H. "Flying Into the Big-City Airport," _Flying_, LXXIV (March 1964), 26-29.

Schechner, William. "The Untouchables: Mob Scene in Jersey," _Commonweal_, LXXXIX (January 24, 1969), 515-15.

Schein, Bernard. "Newark Experiments with Films," _Wilson Library Bulletin_, XIX (December 1944), 276-77.

Sheerin, John B. "The Meaning of the Newark Riots," _Catholic World_, CCV (September 1967), 105-07.

"Sick, Sick City Looks for a Cure," _Business Week_, (December 27, 1969), 16-17.

"62 Motor Busses With Trolley Poles at Newark," _The American City_, L (February 1935), 69.

"Snow Removal Organization in Newark, N.J." _The American City_, XXVIII (Feburary 1923), 123-24.

Snyder, John P. "The Bounds of Newark: Tract, Township and City," _New Jersey History_, LXXXVI, no. 2 (Summer 1968), 93-105.

"Sold After Sixteen Years; Old Post-Office Site," _Business Week_, (November 28, 1953), 150.

"Sparks & Tinder," _Time_, XC (July 21, 1967), 15-21.

"Spirit of Newark, U.S.A." _America_, CXVII (July 29, 1967), 105.

Star, J. "All-American Cities; National Municipal League and Look Citations," _Look_, XIX (February 8, 1955), 77.

Steinberg, David. "Newarker Speaks Up for 'Noork,'" _New York Times Magazine_, (October 20, 1963), 99-100.

Stern, Caroline K.   "Creative Ballet," Recreation, XLVII
     (February 1954), 104-06.

"Strike: Newark Ledger Case," News-Week, V (March 23,
     1935), 23.

Sumner, Mary B.   "When a Women's Workroom Burns," The
     Survey, XXV (January 7, 1911), 558-62.

"10-Million Capacity Planned for Newark," Aviation Week
     & Space Technology, LXXXI (November 16, 1964), 37.

"Torch in a Tinderbox," Time, XCI (May 3, 1968), 23.

"Tribute by Business; 50th Anniversary of Newark's
     Business Library," The Library Journal, LXXIX
     (November 1, 1954), 2066.

"Turning a Canal Into a Subway," Literary Digest, CXII
     (January 9, 1932), 30.

"University of Newark," School and Society, XLII (Novem-
     ber 9, 1935), 638.

"Venice Brought to Newark," Literary Digest, LIII (Au-
     gust 26, 1916), 459.

"Visible Man; K. Gibson's Mayoral Victory," Time, XCV
     (June 29, 1970), 12-13.

Ward, William R.   "The Newark Charter Centennial," Pro-
     ceedings of the New Jersey Historical Society, LIV
     (July 1936), 218-33.

Weingast, David E.   "A New Way in Newark: Doing Something
     About Labor Management Relations," Education, LXXII
     (April 1952), 526-30.

Werber, Margaret P.   "Making the Most of a Museum," Na-
     tional Parent-Teacher, XLVIII (March 1954), 33.

Wheeler, M. P.   "How Newark Stands in Unemployment Re-
     lief," Survey, LXVIII (May 15, 1932), 205.

"'Where Are They Now?'; A Year After Riots," Newsweek,
     LXXII (July 29, 1968), 13.

Whitehead, Ralph.   "Newark Riot Report's Missing Ingre-
     dient," New Republic, CLVIII (March 2, 1968), 12-13.

"Why Business Plane Traffic Is Booming at Newark Air Ser-
     vice," Flying, LXVI (March 1960), 42-43.

UNPUBLISHED STUDIES

Bennett, Hugh F. "A History of the University of Newark, 1908-1946." Doctoral dissertation, New York University, 1956.

Blaker, Cynthia G. "Newark Mechanics Association: A Lyceum in 1828." Master's thesis, Fairleigh Dickinson University, 1964.

Bloomberg, Susan. "Industrialization and Skilled Workers: Newark, 1826 to 1860." Doctoral dissertation, University of Michigan, 1974.

Cato, Revis D. "Discharging of Federal Funds for Low-Income Housing in the City of Newark." Master's thesis, Montclair State College, 1973.

Decter, Stephen A. "The Politics of Municipal Charter Revision: Newark, New Jersey, 1947-1953." Senior thesis, Princeton University, 1959.

Douglas, Philip LeB. "Reform in Newark: The Response to Crisis, 1953-1972." Senior thesis, Princeton University, 1972.

Galishoff, Stuart. "Public Health in Newark, 1832-1918." Doctoral dissertation, New York University, 1969.

Hinrichsen, Carl D. "The History of the Diocese of Newark, 1873-1901." Doctoral dissertation, The Catholic University of America, 1963.

Kaplan, Harold. "The Politics of Slum Clearance. A Study of Urban Renewal in Newark, New Jersey." Doctoral dissertation, Columbia University, 1961.

Kussick, Marilyn R. "Social Reform As a Tool of Urban Reform: The Emergence of the Twentieth-Century Public School in Newark, New Jersey, 1890-1920." Doctoral dissertation, Rutgers University, 1974.

Loffredo, Carmine A. "A History of the Roman Catholic School System in the Archdiocese of Newark, New Jersey, 1900-1964." Doctoral dissertation, Rutgers University, 1967.

Moore, Lester L. "A History of the Professional Theatre in Newark, New Jersey, From 1847 to 1867." Doctoral dissertation, Columbia University, 1966.

Paige, Jeffrey M. "Collective Violence and the Culture of Subordination: A Study of Participants in the

July 1967 Riots in Newark, New Jersey, and Detroit,
Michigan." Doctoral dissertation, University of
Michigan, 1968.

Peckarsky, Anita. "A Study of the Family Health Care
Unit in the Model Cities Area of Newark." Master's
thesis, Montclair State College, 1973.

Popper, Samuel H. "Newark, N. J., 1870-1910: Chapters
in the Evolution of an American Metropolis." Doctoral dissertation, New York University, 1952.

Rubinfeld, William A. "An Appraisal of Guidance Services
of the Newark Secondary Schools Through a Follow-up
Study of Selected School Leavers." Doctoral dissertation, New York University, 1960.

Sabine, Julia E. "Antecedents of the Newark Public Library: A Study of Books and Readers in Newark,
1666-1889." Doctoral dissertation, The University
of Chicago, 1946.

Schnall, Kenneth. "A Survey of Ecclesiastical Architecture Built in Newark from 1810-1865." Master's
thesis, Kean College of New Jersey, 1965.

Spiegel, Marshall. "Newark: From the Drama of Its
Founding to the Drama of Its First Playwright."
Master's thesis, Fairleigh Dickinson University,
1961.

Strauss, William D. "An Analysis of the Problems Faced
by Merchants in Newark's Riot-torn Central Ward."
Master's thesis, Fairleigh Dickinson University,
1969.

Testa, James A. "The Italians of Newark: The Process of
Economic Victory and Social Retreat, 1910-1940."
Senior thesis, Princeton University, 1970.

Turp, Ralph K. "Public Schools in the City of Newark,
New Jersey: 1850-1965." Doctoral dissertation,
Rutgers University, 1967.

NO POSTAGE
NECESSARY
IF MAILED
IN THE
UNITED STATES

BUSINESS REPLY MAIL
FIRST-CLASS MAIL   PERMIT NO. 113   MT MORRIS IL

POSTAGE WILL BE PAID BY ADDRESSEE

SUBSCRIPTIONS SERVICE DEPT.
PO BOX 509
MT. MORRIS IL 61054-7763

THE REAL ACTION STARTS IN...

FREE PREVIEW ISSUE
of SHONEN JUMP Magazine!

THE WORLD'S MOST POPULAR MANGA

Each issue of SHONEN JUMP contains the coolest manga available in the U.S., anime news, and info on video & card games, toys AND more!

50% OFF THE PRICE

Get your FREE Preview Issue!

ST SUB CLUB Benefits

ACCESS exclusive areas of *www.shonenjump.com*

ALWAYS get every issue

RECEIVE free members-only gifts

Tell us what you think about SHONEN JUMP manga!
Our survey is now available online.
Go to: www.SHONENJUMP.com/mangasurvey
Help us make our product offering better!
THE REAL ACTION STARTS IN...
SHONEN JUMP
THE WORLD'S MOST POPULAR MANGA
www.shonenjump.com
SJ ADVANCED
SJ
viz media
BLEACH © 2001 by Tite Kubo/SHUEISHA Inc. NARUTO © 1999 by Masashi Kishimoto/SHUEISHA Inc.
DEATH NOTE © 2003 by Tsugumi Ohba, Takeshi Obata/SHUEISHA Inc. ONE PIECE © 1997 by Eiichiro Oda/SHUEISHA Inc.

VIZ
MEDIA
www.viz.com

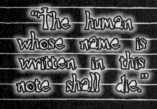

"The note shall become the property of the human world, once it touches the ground of (arrives in) the human world."

It has arrived.

THEN LET'S YOU AND I GO TOGETHER!

TO GUN BLAZE WEST!!

BROTHER...

EH?

CHK CHK

OIL

THUD

SMIRK

...RIGHT NOW, I...

...CAN'T GO.

NO...

"Yes. Something that strongly captivates men's hearts…

As it is passed down between people, it takes on the form of their expectations and hopes, eventually turning into legend."

"Truth?"

"Understand, Will, there is always some truth behind what we call legend."

"I'm going …!"

"No… I think it'll be too much for you, Carol."

"Ahh! I'm going, too!"

"Can I?"

"Will, will you come search with me when you grow up—for Gun Blaze West?"

…BELIEVING THAT IT MAY HAVE BEEN A KIND OF COLISEUM OF THE ANCIENT NATIVES.

GUN BLAZE WEST

BASED ON THE LEGEND THAT SAID "ONLY THE STRONG ARE ALLOWED TO SET FOOT IN GUN BLAZE WEST," FATHER CONDUCTED RESEARCH…

DON'T GO ON ABOUT SUCH UNNECESSARY THINGS.

CAROL.

BROTHER CARRIED ON THE RESEARCH IN THE HOPES THAT ONE DAY, WITHOUT FAIL, HE WOULD…

…YOUR GOAL IS ALSO TO HEAD WEST FOR GUN BLAZE WEST.

I SEE…

182

...I DON'T RECALL THAT.

TEE-HEE

...YOU WERE JUMPING WITH JOY, TOO, BROTHER! IT WAS QUITE A SIGHT.

WHAT'RE YOU TALKING ABOUT? WHEN YOU FIRST FIGURED OUT HOW IT WORKED...

...THAT COMPASS OF YOURS ALSO...!

THAT WOULD MEAN...

...IF YOUR GUN HAS THE SAME...

MORE IMPORTANTLY...

TA-DA!

IT POINTS WEST!!

THIS COMPASS... THE NEEDLE DOESN'T POINT NORTH.

OH... SO THIS IS A COMPASS?

BUT IT'S NOT YOUR USUAL TYPE. LOOK CLOSELY.

CLICK

LET'S GET DOWN TO BUSINESS.

TMP

ARE YOU AN IDIOT?

HEE HEE

WHAT A DISCOVERY! A MAGICAL COMPASS!!

This way, when the bottom needle points north, the needle above will of course point west.

The two needles are set at 90 degree angels.

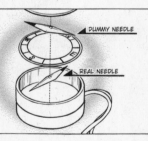

DUMMY NEEDLE

REAL NEEDLE

It's not magic or anything like that. The needle that points west is just for show. The real needle, made of magnetic material, is hidden under the compass face.

IT'S NOTHING TO BE AMAZED BY OR TO GET HAPPY ABOUT.

WITH A LITTLE THOUGHT, EVEN A CHILD COULD HAVE FIGURED IT OUT.

IT SOUNDS LIKE YOU'RE MOCKING ME.

STOP IT.

OH... YOU'RE AWESOME! SMART!

...BUT WHEN YOU SAW THIS, YOU REACTED JUST LIKE ME.

I THOUGHT HE WAS NOTHING BUT A STOIC, BORING DUDE...

GRIN

AWESOME! A HOUSE BUILT OF SOD!

Outskirts of St. Louis

BROTHER, STOP THAT.

THESE DAYS, IT'S JUST A PAUPER'S HOUSE THAT KEEPS THE RAIN AWAY.

BUT IT'S AWESOME! WAY TO GO PIONEERS!!

IT'S A HOUSE CONCEIVED BY THE OLD PIONEERS OF THE GREAT PLAINS WHERE MATERIALS WERE IN SHORT SUPPLY.

THIS IS CALLED A GRASS HOUSE.

I HAVE NO INTENTION OF LIVING LONG!

...YOU'LL DIE AN EARLY DEATH.

...I'VE BEEN PREPARED TO RISK MY LIFE!

GU!!

EVER SINCE THE DAY I WAS GIVEN THIS...

!!

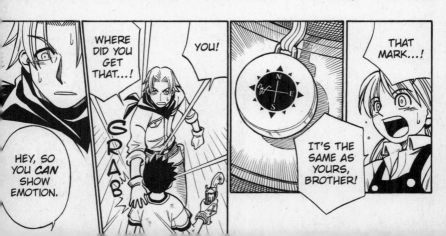

WHERE DID YOU GET THAT...!

YOU!

HEY, SO YOU CAN SHOW EMOTION.

GRAB

THAT MARK...!

IT'S THE SAME AS YOURS, BROTHER!

BROTHER!

THINK A BIT MORE BEFORE YOU ACT, OR ELSE YOU'LL REGRET IT DURING YOUR TRAVELS.

! TMP

IT'S HIS FAULT FOR BEING SO EASILY GOADED INTO A FIGHT.

THAT WON'T BE NECESSARY. THAT YOUNG MAN GOT WHAT HE DESERVED.

!

THEY ALSO MADE FUN OF BOSS'S FOOD!

THOSE GUYS MADE FUN OF CAROL'S WORDS OF SUPPORT!

I'M NOT SMART...

...SO I'LL TAKE ON ANYBODY WHO WANTS A FIGHT!!

BELLA DONNA
SALOON

BELLADONNA IS MY PRECIOUS CASTLE.

THE MORE "KNIGHTS" WE HAVE TO ADD COLOR TO THE CASTLE, THE BETTER IT LOOKS.

THAT'S ALL IT IS.

YOU'RE NOT THINKING...

...THAT HE'S STRONGER THAN ME, I HOPE?

HEY, CARLO.

IT'S JUST THAT THAT A LASSO-WIELDING BOUNCER WOULD BE GOOD FOR ATTRACTING CUSTOMERS.

NOT AT ALL.

...are of the same rank and equal?!

In other words, his lasso skills and my gun...

NOW, NOW, YOU TWO.

MY SALOON IS IN SHAMBLES!

HOW SO?!

IT WAS SHABBY TO BEGIN WITH SO DON'T WORRY ABOUT IT!

SHFF

ARE YOU INJURED? ANYWAY, LET'S GO BACK INSIDE...

THE MATTER IS CLOSED!!

OKAY!

TA-DA!

174

CHAPTER·7:
WILLJOHNSTON

CHARACTER INTRODUCTIONS
AND EXTRAS WILL BE
INCLUDED AS OF VOLUME 2.

SORRY.

I'M GOING WEST!!

SHOOOO

DOOM

I TOLD YOU...

...I HAVE TOUGH LEGS.

HE LIFTED THAT BIG OLD TABLE AS IF IT WERE NOTHING...

THERE ARE ALL KINDS OF GUNS, I SUPPOSE.

SHOOOO...

BUT THOSE TINY BULLETS SCATTERED THE MOMENT THEY WERE FIRED...

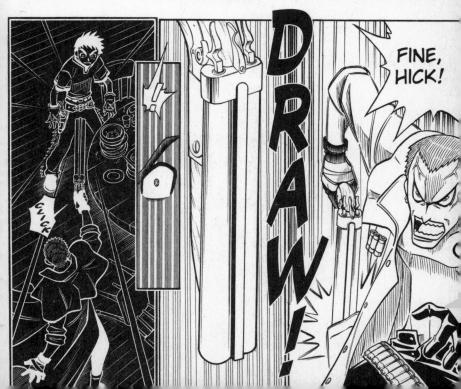

THE BEST NEXT TO CISSY'S.

IT'S DELICIOUS.

...TASTES AWFUL, RIGHT?

THE FOOD HERE...

THAT'S WHAT YOU CALL HARASSMENT...!

WHAM!

ST. LOUIS IS THE GATEWAY TO THE WEST, SO I'VE SEEN DOZENS AND DOZENS OF KIDS LIKE YOU TRYING TO HEAD WEST...

...BUT ALMOST ALL OF THEM HIGHTAILED IT BACK HOME CRYING WITH THEIR TAILS BETWEEN THEIR LEGS.

IS THAT SO? THEN FOR YOUR OWN GOOD, HIGHTAIL IT BACK TO CISSY'S PLACE.

YOUR TOUGH GUY ACT DOESN'T PLAY HERE—SAVE THAT FOR YOUR HICK HOMETOWN!!

KIDS WHO MISTAKENLY THINK THEY'RE STRONG CAN'T GO WEST!

IF YOU DON'T, YOU'LL JOIN THE UNDERDOGS.

YEAH. I GOT TOUGH LEGS.

YOU RAN HERE?!

ILLINOIS? THAT'S QUITE FAR AWAY.

AAHH!!

WINSTON TOWN, ILLINOIS.

I'M CURIOUS... WHERE ARE YOU FROM, VIU?

NAW, IT'S NOT THAT FAR. YOU JUST GOTTA SLEEP, THEN RUN, THEN DO IT ALL OVER AGAIN.

SO, NEXT YOU'RE GOING TO RUN TO THE WEST, I SUPPOSE.

IT'S NOT A LIE.

SOUNDS LIKE YOU'RE LYING...

MY OLDER BROTHER SAYS HE'S GOING WEST SOMEDAY, TOO.

A LOT OF MEN ARE LIKE THAT.

...COULD BOTH GET THERE!

IT'D BE NICE IF THE TWO OF YOU...

TO PREPARE, HE'S BEEN STUDYING AND STUDYING EVERY SINGLE DAY...

...IT'S ALREADY BEEN TEN YEARS.

I HAVEN'T INTRODUCED MYSELF YET.

I'M CAROL.

YUM!!

SCARF SCARF

SCARF

MUNCH MUNCH

OOH!

CHOMP CHOMP CHOMP

GOBBLE GOBBLE

NO!

IT MUST BE BECAUSE YOU'RE SUCH A WEIRD CHARACTER, BOSS.

BUT IF THE FOOD'S THIS GOOD AND YOUR PLACE STILL ISN'T POPULAR,

SO YOU ADMIT THAT IT'S AMAZING?

UH-HUH

BFOSS (BOSS), THIS IS TOPS!

AS A RESULT, OUR CUSTOMERS HAVE COMPLETELY LEFT US OVER THE PAST HALF-YEAR.

THAT SCUMBAG OF AN OWNER ACROSS THE STREET SAYS WE'RE AN EYESORE, SO HE HIRED NOTORIOUS OUTLAWS TO HARASS US FOR EVERY LITTLE THING!

SALOON

IT'S THAT SALOON ACROSS THE STREET, "BELLA-DONNA"!

LATELY, DECENT LOCAL FOLK WON'T COME NEAR, SO NOW THOSE GUYS PREY UPON THE TRAVELERS GOING TO AND FROM THE WEST.

SINCE THAT SALOON WAS BUILT, THE STREET HAS GOTTEN PRETTY DANGEROUS.

THEY RIP OFF THEIR CUSTOMERS, BRAWL-ANYTHING THEY WANT.

CHEW

154

This is how Viu would test...

...how strong he was.

Viu's...

..."trial" began.

The setting: the American West

His goal: Gun Blaze West

CHAPTER 6:

THE TRIAL BEGINS

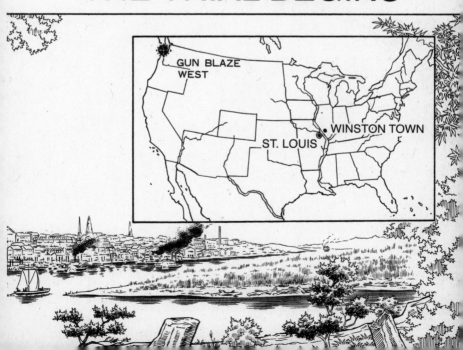

WELL...

...I'LL BE HEADING

...FOR A WHILE!!

TA-DA!

IT'S NOT A SIGHTSEEING TRIP!

I WANT SOME CALIFORNIA GOLD JEWELRY.

GRRRR

TEXAS BEEF JERKY FOR ME.

BRING BACK A SOUVENIR!

YES. FROM "THAT DAY" FIVE YEARS AGO...

...I KNEW VIU WOULD SET OUT LIKE THIS ON A JOURNEY ONE DAY.

BLAH

ARE YOU SURE ABOUT THIS, CISSY?

THEN WHAT ARE YOU GOING FOR?

WHAT? THAT SUCKS.

WHAT DO YOU MEAN "THAT SUCKS"?

BLAH

I'VE GOT IT-TREASURE HUNTING!

BLAH

CHAPTER 6:
THE TRIAL BEGINS

Viu Bannes, at fourteen years old, completes his training!!

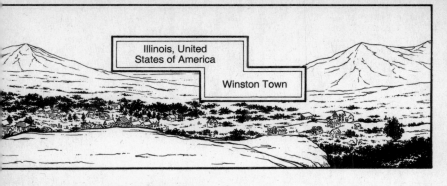

Illinois, United States of America

Winston Town

The year 1880.

...Viu began his training alone.

On the next day...

NNNG!

Days and months go by and seasons pass
as our story moves to five years later.

... MARCUS ...!

MARCUS ...!

WHAAAAA!

And so...

...Viu and Marcus' friendship came to an end after just ten days.

NO! NOT YET!

— Don't cry. —

DON'T SET YET!

DON'T SET!!

— Aren't you strong? Weren't you going to become stronger? —

— Then you mustn't cry over something like this. —

DON'T SET !!

...let's become stronger!!

Together...

Use it wisely.

I'm going to let you borrow my life.

If you run away then, you'll be running from your top priority!

...and go the place we dreamt of!

Let's become strong...

But! When you absolutely have to fight, fight absolutely!!

I won't let you, Friend.

You can't go on ahead alone.

TSK TSK

!! AAAGH!

SHOOM

GRRR!

THUNK

138

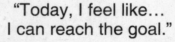

"Today, I feel like…
I can reach the goal."

If we can make it to that high rock
before the sun sets, we'll set out together.

We'll set out… together.

There is…a map.

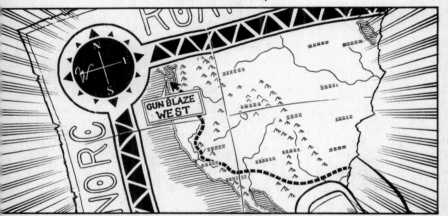

The map is my only clue to Gun Blaze West.

134

WHOOMP

MOVE ASIDE!

HFF

MARCUS ISN'T AN UNDER-DOG...

AND I'M NOT GOING TO BECOME AN UNDER-DOG...

HFF

WHAT THE—?!

CHIK

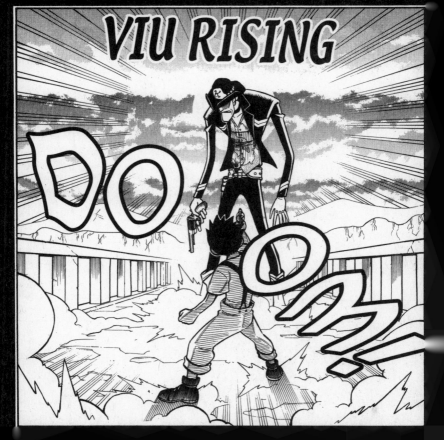

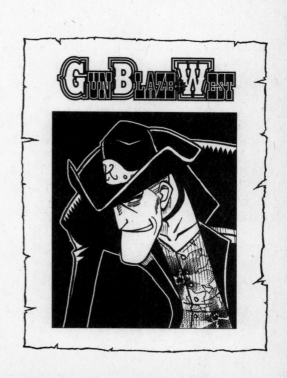

WHOOSH SPL ASH

GET LOST...

...YOU "UNDERDOG."

MARCUS HOMER!

WHA...?

OH!

MARCUS!!

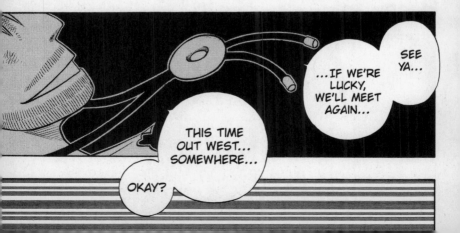

SEE YA...

...IF WE'RE LUCKY, WE'LL MEET AGAIN...

THIS TIME OUT WEST... SOMEWHERE...

OKAY?

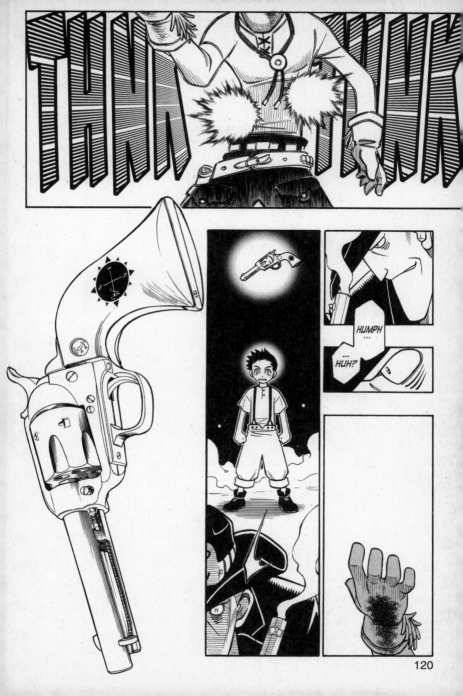

SHF...

I AIN'T DOWN YET...

NOT SO FAST, YOU TWO...

WOBBLE

THAT WAS CLOSE. REAL CLOSE...

TSK.

ANNOYING PUNK ...

PLIP...

PLIP...

PLIP...

BAM

BAM

114

110

CHAPTER 4:
MARCUS FADES OUT

SMOKE!!

RARGH!

TMP TMP TMP

HFF HFF HFF HFF HFF

BA!! SHООМ

HFF HFF

CHAPTER 4:
MARCUS FADES OUT

THERE MIGHT BE OTHERS STILL HIDING SOMEWHERE.

DON'T GET CARRIED AWAY, MAGGOTS.

FOR EXAMPLE...

SHAA...

...IN THAT CABIN.

HURRY, FRIEND! CISSY AND THE OTHERS ARE IN DANGER!

HFF

HFF

HFF

HFF

HFF

RIGHT!

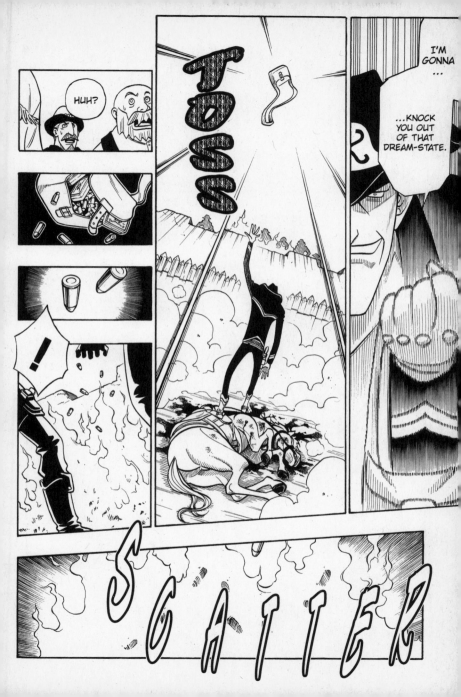

98

HMPH... THE REINFORCEMENTS FROM CHICAGO DIDN'T MAKE IT IN TIME.

A COUNTRY SHERIFF AND A BUNCH OF AMATEURS IS ALL THEY HAVE.

THEY'RE WAITING IN AMBUSH.

SIX OR SEVEN OF THEM.

CLIPPITY CLOP

THERE'S NO NEED TO EVEN USE OUR GUNS!

RRA

RGH!

YOU MEN TAKE YOUR TIME AND FOLLOW ME!

CHIK

CHAK

CLIPPITY-CLOPPITY-CLOP

!

A ONE-MAN ATTACK?!

CALM DOWN. GET READY TO FIRE.

TA-DA

THE PATH WE RAN WAS THE WEST TRAIL THAT WAS MENTIONED THE OTHER DAY...

I SEE.

SO THIS IS THAT CHECKPOINT IN THE VALLEY THEY TALKED ABOUT.

NOT "WHAT". IT'S DANGEROUS HERE.

WHAT?!

ANYWAY, ALL TRAFFIC HAS BEEN STOPPED BEYOND THIS POINT. YOU TWO SHOULD HEAD BACK.

IT'S QUITE REMARKABLE, THOUGH, RUNNING THIS FAR AT HIS AGE.

SHFF SHFF

I'M SORRY, SHERIFF, FOR ALL THE TROUBLE VIU CAUSES.

LET'S STOP HERE TODAY.

WE HAVE NO CHOICE, FRIEND.

ONCE THEY'RE HERE, THEY'LL TAKE CARE OF THE VILLAINS QUICKLY, AND WE'LL BE SAFE.

TODAY IS DAY SEVEN. REINFORCEMENTS FROM CHICAGO WILL BE ARRIVING TOMORROW.

!

HE HAS A FUTURE AS A...

...

OKAY?

NOW I CAN FIRE A GUN!

I DID IT! I PASSED UP MARCUS!

RRRAGH!

VOOE

YEAH!

YOU PAY FOR YOUR OWN, OF COURSE.

WHAT ABOUT THE COST OF BULLETS?

YOU DID IT, FRIEND! FROM TOMORROW, WE'LL ADD SHOOTIN' TRAINING!

!

TIGHT-WAD!

VIU!

AND MARCUS... WHAT'RE YOU DOING HERE?

CISSY...

WHAT'RE YOU DOING HERE?

DIDN'T I TELL YOU THIS MORNING THAT I HAD DUTY SO I'D BE HOME LATE TONIGHT?

WHY? BECAUSE IT'S MY JOB TO FEED THE TOWN VOLUNTEERS.

HYUUU

I'M AIMING FOR GUN BLAZE WEST!

WE'LL SET OUT TOGETHER!

I'M AIMING FOR THE WEST.

RIGHT!

RUN!

RUN.

GOOD, FRIEND!

WHIZZZ

CAN'T STOP TO PEE!

HUH?

DANCE.

DANCE!

BAD, FRIEND!

GRUNT

OR EVEN TO POOP...

CONSIDER EVEN THE PRESIDENT YOUR ENEMY!

RIGHT, MARCUS!

CLENCH

THE SCHOOL BELL WILL BE OUR STARTING SIGNAL.

....AND HEAD WEST UNTIL THE SUN SETS.

HFF   HFF   HFF

WE'LL RUN ALONG THIS ROAD...

...AND IF IT CAN MAKE TO THAT HIGH ROCK BEFORE THE SUN SETS...

EVERY DAY, EVERY DAY, WE'LL AIM FOR ONE STEP FURTHER...

OH...

MARCUS, THEY'RE SWOLLEN!

fwip fwip

...WE'RE TRAINING OUR ARMS AS WELL!

NOT JUST OUR FEET, FRIEND?

BLORF

MARCUS, I PUKED!

PUKE...

THAT'LL GIVE US THE NUTRITION WE NEED!

WE'LL SNACK AS WE RUN!

...THIS IS WHAT HAPPENS TO ANYONE WHO GETS IN THE WAY OF OUR GOING WEST.

UNDERSTAND THIS, FRIEND...

92

THAT HIGH ROCK WHERE THE SUN IS SETTING!

THAT'LL BE OUR "GOAL FOR A NEW BEGINNING"!

OF COURSE IT IS. YOU CAN'T CALL IT TRAINING IF IT'S EASY TO REACH.

WOW, THAT'S FAR!

SO...

TAP

...WE'LL USE A STONE TO MARK HOW FAR WE'VE RUN EACH DAY.

TAP

THE NEXT DAY, JUST A BIT FARTHER THAN THIS STONE.

THE DAY AFTER, A BIT FARTHER THAN THAT STONE.

TAP

IN THIS WAY, EVERY DAY...

91

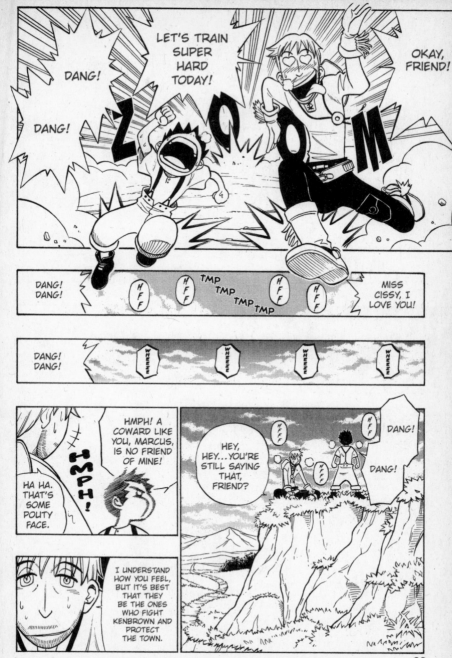

88

WAIT! HE'S AN OUTSIDER!

ISN'T IT TOO RISKY TO INCLUDE SOMEONE WE KNOW NOTHING ABOUT?

HEY, WHAT ABOUT ME?!

CLNK

CLNK

CLNK

RIGHT! MARCUS IS A PRO WITH A GUN.

HE'LL BE A POWERFUL HELP.

CLNK

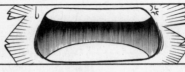

VIU!

AND I HAVE TO GET MY GUN BELT BACK!

I FOUGHT THE KENBROWN GANG, TOO, DIDN'T I?!

PHEW...

I...

YOU STAY AT HOME AND BEHAVE YOURSELF.

IT'S OKAY, DON'T FORCE YOURSELF. WHAT THE SHERIFF SAYS MAKES SENSE.

I WANTED TO JOIN THE FIGHT.

DARN IT.

AS FOR MARCUS, I THOUGHT ABOUT THAT LAST NIGHT.

I THINK WE TOWNSFOLK SHOULD TAKE CARE OF OUR TOWN ALONE.

LEAVE THE TOWN'S AFFAIRS TO US AND PLAY TOGETHER WITH VIU INSTEAD.

PLEASE.

THIS IS NO PLACE FOR CHILDREN ANYMORE.

CHAPTER 3:
KENBROWN ATTACKS

OK. I'LL GIVE YOU A HANDICAP. I'LL FORBID THE USE OF THAT SURE-FIRE TECHNIQUE.

YEAH, BUT IF YOU USE THAT SKUNK TRICK AGAIN, WE'RE FINISHED!

THEN SHALL WE GET TO TRAINING?

OKAY!

RIGHT!

OH YEAH, LET'S SEE...

TMP

WHAT ABOUT A FINISH LINE? WHAT'LL IT BE?

OKAY! READY.

I'VE GOT IT. HOW ABOUT ONE STEP FARTHER THAN YESTERDAY.

START!

WILL YOU REALLY TEACH ME HOW TO SHOOT A GUN?

YEAH, BUT ONLY IF YOU CAN PASS ME IN A RACE.

OH, AND KEEP THIS AN ABSOLUTE SECRET FROM MISS CISSY.

REALLY?

IF YOU DON'T SNAP IT UP, YOU MIGHT END UP DEAD BEFORE YOU EVER HEAD WEST.

AS MISS CISSY SAYS, GUNS AREN'T NECESSARY FOR CHILDREN, AND IT WOULD BE BEST IF ADULTS DIDN'T NEED THEM EITHER.

LET'S GET GOING TO "THE PLACE YOU DREAMT OF"!

...I'LL ADD YOU TO MY SOFA.

IF THIS ISN'T THE LAST TIME THAT KIND OF BULL HAPPENS...

...WILL BE KILLED!

VIU AND MARCUS, AND ANYONE WHO DEFIES US...

DOOM!

BUT ALL I HAVE IS THAT GUN BELT!

MARCUS HAS A GUN AND THE MAP!

TO VIU, A GUN AND GUN BELT ARE IMPORTANT ITEMS FOR GOING WEST.

EVEN IF HE BECOMES STRONG, WITHOUT THEM, HE'S...

NOW I SEE...

HOW CAN I BE A MAN IF I JUST HANG AROUND AND DO NOTHING?

VIU!

I'VE GOT TO FIGURE OUT SOME WAY TO GET A GUN.

FWIP

...SO?

AND THEN YOU CAME BACK WITHOUT YOUR WEAPONS?

...TOOK YOU FOR A RIDE?

SO THAT FILTHY GUN-SLINGER AND KID...

YOU GUYS ARE HORSING AROUND?!

SO... WHILE I'M SWEATIN' BEING PURSUED BY AN ARKANSAS POSSE...

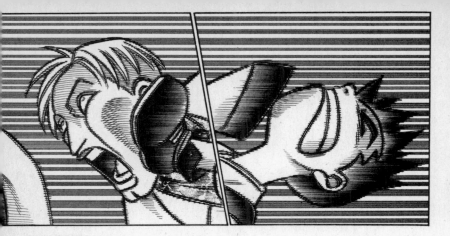

DANG...

WHO IS THAT SON OF A...

THUNK

77

74

THIS TIME FOR SURE I'M GETTING MY GUN BELT BACK!

OKAY!

CLENCH

WE'VE GOT A PROBLEM.

IT WOULD SEEM SO!

KENBROWN'S COMING TO THIS TOWN?

THAT'S WHAT I LIKE ABOUT YOU, BUT THIS TIME I THINK YOU SHOULD FORGET IT, FRIEND.

WHY?

STOP IT! PLEASE! JUST STOP IT!

BOOM!!

YOU DON'T GET IT, DO YOU, FRIEND. MEN ARE POWERLESS IN THE FACE OF LOVE.

THAT'S NOT FAIR, MARCUS! YOU CALL YOURSELF A MAN?!

WHAP

POW

STOP YOUR FIGHTING AND GET SOME SLEEP.

WE'RE GETTING AN EARLY START TOMORROW MORNING.

ANYTHING FOR YOU, MISS CISSY. ♡

BLUSH ♡

BLUSH

BLUSH

BLUSH

BLUSH

MARCUS, PLEASE DON'T EVER LET THIS CHILD HOLD A GUN, OKAY?

WHAT ?!

OKAY! BEDTIME!

MAKE SURE YOU TAKE A BATH FIRST.

MISS CISSY, SHALL I WASH YOUR BACK FOR YOU?

NO THANK YOU.

OKAY! WE'LL GO!

TOMORROW MORNING, THEY'RE ESCORTING THE TWO OUTLAWS YOU CAPTURED THE OTHER DAY.

THE SHERIFF SAYS HE HAS SOMETHING TO TELL US SO HE WANTS US THERE.

WON'T YOU COME?

68

THERE WAS A BIG COMMOTION A WHILE BACK WHEN TWO OUTLAWS WERE CAPTURED ON THE DAY OF THE HARVEST FESTIVAL.

NOT LATELY.

WELL, SOMETHING LIKE THAT.

IT'S A NICE, QUIET TOWN HERE.

WEL-COME.

YOU A PEDDLER?

...AND WHILE YOU'RE AT IT, TELL ME MORE ABOUT THIS STORY.

FIX ME SOMETHING LIGHT TO EAT...

HFF HFF HFF HFF HFF HFF HFF HFF HFF HFF

FOUL! TOO FOUL!

HA HA HA!

I'M TAKING THE LEAD FROM THE TOP, FRIEND!

ZOOM

ISN'T IT VIU-TIFUL?!

YOU SKUNKY JERK!

HEY VIU, YOU LOSER BUTT!

MARCUS, YOU SKUNK!

TMP TMP TMP TMP TMP TMP TMP

Winston Town

[SALOON]

UUUY...

TMP TMP

WHAT ?!

TMP

SHUT UP!

TMP TMP

CLIPPITY CLOP

GUNSLINGER MARCUS!

OKAY! WHERE'S THE TARGET?

HA!

FWIP FWIP

HEY, HEY. WHO SAID WE'D BE DOING ANY SHOOTING?

OKAY!

WE'LL BEGIN OUR TRAINING HERE.

FIRST, WE'LL BEGIN WITH BASIC CONDITIONING.

NO.

AWW MAN...

NO SHOOTING?!

IT'S TOO EARLY TO BEGIN SHOOTING WITH YOUR TINY HANDS.

OH...

...YOU WOULDN'T LOOK ME IN THE EYE.

I SEE—I GET IT!

YOU DON'T HAVE MONEY TO BUY BULLETS.

IN A WORD...

"RUNNING."

AND THERE'S AN IDEAL TRAINING METHOD TO DEVELOP BOTH AT THE SAME TIME.

LISTEN, FRIEND, THE BASICS OF STRENGTH ARE STAMINA AND INNER STRENGTH.

IT'S SIMPLE, AND INCREDIBLY EFFECTIVE.

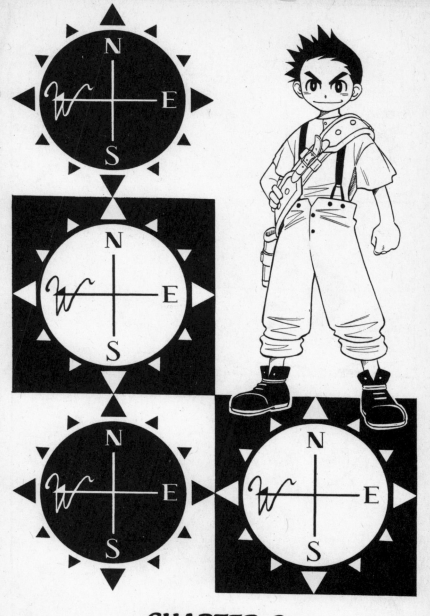

CHAPTER 2:
THE TRAINING BEGINS

...A MAP.

THERE IS...

GENERALLY SPEAKING, SUCH DUBIOUS PLACES HAVE NEVER EXISTED.

EVEN IF BY CHANCE IT DID EXIST, THERE'S NO WAY TO GET THERE WITHOUT A MAP SHOWING YOU ITS LOCATION.

THE MAN WHO DEFEATED THE BAD OUTLAW WITH VIU!

YAY! YA—

OH! IT'S MARCUS!

MARCUS!

MARCUS!!

YAY!

YEAH!

YAY!

YEAH!

BACK TO YOUR SEATS, EVERYONE!

LET'S SEE IT!

MARCUS, YOU HAVE A MAP?

YES!

NOPE!

NOO

...!

I'M NOT BEING STINGY.

STINGY!

SIGH... WE BARELY MANAGED TO SURVIVE.

I THOUGHT WE WERE DEAD, FOR SURE.

HFF

HFF WHEEZE

WHEEZE

HFF

WHEEZE

HFF WHEEZE

AWW MAN! MY GUNBELT...!

GRRR!

WHAT? YOU WERE LISTENING? BUT I DON'T RECALL EVER TELLING YOU I WAS STRONG.

UNLIKE YOU.

WHAT WAS THAT "UNDER-DOG MARCUS" ABOUT?!

YOU'RE BEAT UP, TOO!

HEH-HEH. YOU LOOK REAL BEAT UP, FRIEND.

IT'S SPECIAL TRAINING STARTING TOMORROW!

DANG IT! I'M GOING TO BECOME STRONGER!

YES, I'M SURE OF IT.

CISSY, IS IT TRUE? DID VIU REALLY SAY THE KEN-BROWN GANG?

CLOPPITY-CLOP

HFF

HFF

DANG! KEN-BROWN IS A FAMOUS AND HEINOUS OUTLAW...

...WITH A BOUNTY ON HIS HEAD.

!

WHA?!

IF HE'S FIGHTING A GANG LIKE THAT...

DOOM

...GIVE IT BACK...!

HFF

HFF

MY... GUN BELT...

MY GUN BELT ...

HFF

HFF

IT'S NOT HERE ANYMORE.

OH, TOO BAD ABOUT THAT.

...I HANDED IT TO HIM, AS A PRESENT FOR THE BOSS.

WHEN A MEMBER OF THE GANG CAME TO CONTACT US...

FO OM

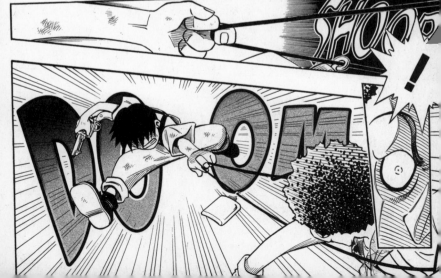

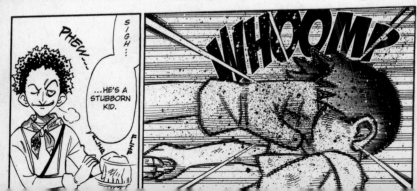

HA HA HA... ...THAT'S FINE WITH ME.

THIS TIME I HAVE NO INTENTION OF RUNNING.

WAS IT TEN YEARS AGO...?

I HEADED WAY OUT WEST TO GET TO "THE PLACE I DREAMT OF."

BUT IN THE VERY FIRST YEAR, I LEARNED HOW INCREDIBLY WEAK I REALLY WAS.

AFTER THAT I RAN FROM EVERYTHING WITH MY TAIL BETWEEN MY LEGS.

PLIP

FROM STRONG GUYS, WEAK GUYS, THE OUTLAW ROUNDUPS...

...AND FROM THE WEST ITSELF...

LAST NIGHT, I HIGHTAILED IT OUT OF THERE, TOO.

PLIP PLIP

PLIP

THAT'S WHY EVERYONE WHO KNOWS ME...

...CALLS ME BY THE NICKNAME...

"UNDERDOG MARCUS."

BUT...

...I'M GIVING UP THAT NAME AS OF TODAY.

I THINK SO, TOO.

IT FITS YOU.

...BUT A KID WITH A TOY GUN ISN'T EVEN WORTH TAKING HOSTAGE.

I DON'T KNOW WHERE YOU TWO BECAME FRIENDS...

HEY!

FWIP FWIP

SHOOP

?!

WHO'D YOU SAY YOUR HOSTAGE WAS?

I'M GOING TO LET YOU BORROW MY LIFE.

YAAAH!!

... USE IT...

...WISELY.

...EASYGOING TOWN.

WHAT A REALLY...

SHFF

FOUND YOU!

TA-DA!

HUH?

THE MORE I LOOK AT IT, THE MORE I WANT TO GO WILD.

I HOPE BOSS AND THE OTHERS GET HERE SOON.

STOMP

HOW STRONG AM I? HOW STRONG CAN I BECOME?

WANTING TO FIND OUT IS A MAN'S BASIC INSTINCT.

...I UNDERSTAND HOW YOU FEEL...

...BUT THIS IS SOMETHING YOU CAN'T DO ANYTHING ABOUT.

PAT

THERE'S REALLY NOTHING YOU CAN DO.

SOME FOOLS KEEP ON WONDERING UNTIL THEY'RE OLD ENOUGH TO GROW SCRUFFY BEARDS.

GRRR!

NO... EVEN IF I HELPED YOU, THOSE TWO WOULD BE TOO MUCH FOR A CHILD TO HANDLE.

I OWE THOSE GUYS, TOO.

JUST A MINUTE, FRIEND.

TMP

THAT'S WHY I'M GOING TO...

...LET YOU BORROW MY LIFE.

YOU'RE GOING TO HELP ME?

VIU,
THAT'S
ENOUGH.

TMP

NO!

TMP

TMP

I'LL BUY
YOU AN
EVEN
NICER
GUN BELT.

VIU, LET
THE
SHERIFF
TAKE CARE
OF THE
REST AND
GO BACK
TO TOWN.

I...

DOOM

...AND
BECOME A
GUNSLINGER
AND
GO WEST!

...ONE
DAY I'M
GOING
TO GET
MY *OWN*
GUN...

...AND PUT
IT IN
MY GUN
BELT...

...WITH
MY TAIL
BETWEEN
MY LEGS!

THERE'S
NO WAY
I'LL RUN
OFF....

36

MISS CISSY?

I'M SORRY...

SNIFF

I DON'T EVER...

...WANT TO LOSE ANOTHER FAMILY MEMBER.

MY PARENTS WERE THE SHERIFF AND DEPUTY OF THIS TOWN, BUT...

...EIGHT YEARS AGO THEY DIED IN THE LINE OF DUTY, SHOT BY AN EVIL GUNSLINGER.

SINCE THEN, I DON'T LIKE ANYTHING THAT HAS TO DO WITH GUNS.

BUT VIU DOESN'T REMEMBER ANYTHING, OF COURSE, BECAUSE HE WAS STILL SMALL, AND...

...HE'S A BOY, SO I LET HIM DO WHAT HE WANTED.

BUT I NEVER IMAGINED SOMETHING LIKE THIS COULD HAPPEN...

!

VIU!

...MUST MEAN THEY HAVE SOMETHING TO DO WITH THE "OUTLAW ROUNDUPS."

THEIR ARKANSAS ACCENTS...

...ARE PROBABLY THE STAGECOACH ROBBERS THE SHERIFF MENTIONED.

HFF

THOSE GUYS WHO SHOT ME OUT OF THE BLUE LAST NIGHT...

HFF

T-MP
T-MP
T-MP

HE'S APPREHENDING EVERY SLIGHTLY SUSPICIOUS GUNSLINGER AND VAGRANT, NOT TO MENTION OUTLAW, AND SENDING THEM ONE AFTER ANOTHER TO THE GALLOWS.

THEIR KIND HAVE BEGUN SCATTERING IN EVERY DIRECTION. THAT'S HOW THOSE GUYS GOT HERE.

A JUDGE FROM A PLACE CALLED FORT SMITH IS LEADING A HUGE OUTLAW ROUNDUP IN THE STATE OF ARKANSAS.

...NO, THIS IS NO TIME TO BE THINKING OF THAT.

DANG. COMING THIS DISTANCE AND STILL MEETING UP WITH MORE OF THEIR KIND MEANS...

ANYWAY, LET'S HURRY! AGAINST A CHILD, EVEN MEN LIKE THEM WOULDN'T...

34

OOH, SUCH A CUTE PUNCH. ♡

MARCUS...

GASP

CAW

HEY, TAP

I DON'T CARE!

ANYWAY, WHERE IS VIU?!

SOME-THING BAD IS GOING ON HERE.

WHY ARE YOU HERE?!

HUH?

IT ISN'T SOMETHING THE KEN-BROWN GANG SHOULD BE DOING. I COULD SURE USE A FIGHT.

YOU'RE BUGGING ME. SHUT UP.

BEING THE VANGUARD* IS A LOUSY JOB. IT'S A WONDER YOU CAN TAKE IT SO SERIOUSLY, BEN.

DANG... GIVE IT BACK.

LET'S GO. WE'LL BE LATE FOR OUR MEETING.

THIS IS PERFECT. I'M TAKING IT.

DIDN'T BOSS WANT A NEW ONE?

...MARCUS...

MY GUN BELT...

OH, THEY'RE JUST CROWS...

...THEIR CRIES GIVE ME THE CREEPS...

OAW OAW

CAW CAW

EEEK!

*VANGUARD: SOLDIERS SENT FROM THE MAIN UNIT TO SECRETLY STUDY ENEMY TERRITORY.

32

I'M HERE, MARCUS! LET'S DUEL!

SILENCE

WAKE UP! COME ON!

ARE YOU ASLEEP? HEY!

SHFF

SHFF

WHAT, KID?

WHAT DO YOU WANT?

DOOM

!

THE GUY'S PROBABLY DEAD. IT WAS DARK, SO I COULDN'T SEE WELL, BUT I SHOT HIM FULL OF BULLETS.

MAR...? OH, YOU MEAN THAT SCRUFFY GUY?

WOW, YOU'RE HUGE.

ARE YOU MARCUS'S FRIEND?

GOODBYE.

GOOD-BYE, MISS CISSY!

DING DONG

...DO YOU KNOW WHERE VIU IS?

BOYS...

I WAS HOPING WE COULD GO TOGETHER TO THE FRUIT VENDOR.

HUH?

VIU?

UH-HUH!

HE'S AT THE HUNTER'S CABIN IN THE FOREST.

VIU DASHED OUT.

BLAH BLAH

BLAH

HA!

BLAH

YEAH

SAID HE'S GOING TO DUEL THE GUNSLINGER HE CAPTURED YESTERDAY.

TMP TMP TMP

HFF

HFF

HFF

HFF

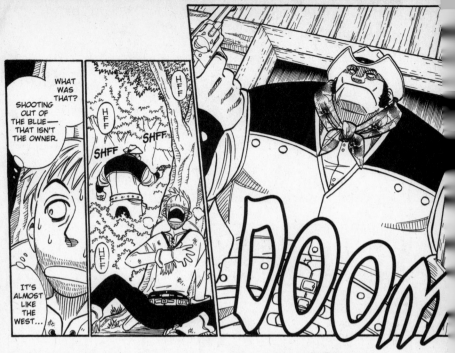

SO WHAT BROUGHT THAT DUDE...

...OUT EAST?

...FROM THE WEST, HE'S LET IT GO TO HIS HEAD!

JUST BECAUSE HE'S A GUN-SLINGER...

TMP TMP TMP

I DON'T WANT TO DUEL A CHILD WITH A TOY PISTOL.

REGARDLESS OF HOW MUCH OF AN "UNDERDOG" I AM,

SKTCH SKTCH

HEY, COME ON, GIVE ME A BREAK.

...GRANTED, IT'S SOMETHING A CHILD WHO KNOWS NOTHING ABOUT THE WEST WOULD SAY.

BUT...

SHOOSH

SHFF

BUT IT'S PROBABLY...

"YOU DON'T KNOW HOW STRONG I AM, DO YOU?!"

EH?

GUESS I HAVE NO CHOICE.

I'LL HIGHTAIL IT OUT OF HERE FIRST THING TOMORROW.

CHEW CHEW

CHOMP CHOMP

NUM NUM NUM

CRUNCH CRUNCH

MUNCH MUNCH

I'LL FIX SUPPER RIGHT AWAY, SO WAIT JUST A LITTLE BIT LONGER...

SORRY I TOOK SO LONG.

WHO ARE YOU?!

OH, FIFFY, FELCOME FOME.

HFF

HFF

KYAAAAAAA!

20

YESTERDAY, THREE COACHES WERE HIT ONE AFTER ANOTHER OVER BEYOND THE WEST ROAD. FIVE GUARDS WERE KILLED.

A STAGECOACH ROBBERY.

WHAT HAPPENED?

...

I DON'T THINK THEY'LL ATTACK THIS TOWN, WHICH HAS NO BANK OR RAILROAD STATION, BUT BE VERY WARY OF STRANGERS.

THEY SAY THE CULPRIT HAD AN ARKANSAS ACCENT, SO IT SEEMS LIKE THE WORK OF A DRIFTER FROM THE WEST.

I'M BACK.

SIGH

I WONDER IF VIU'S HOME LIKE HE SHOULD BE...

...HE DISAPPEARED TOWARDS THE END OF THE FESTIVAL.

CREAK...

TMP

19

NOW GET UP! I SAID DO IT OVER!

UGH...

HE REALLY IS TOUGH.

EVEN "UNDERDOG MARCUS" HAS FALLEN AS LOW AS HE CAN GO.

GRRROWL

I STOLE BECAUSE I WAS SO HUNGRY AND NOW A CHILD APPREHENDS ME.

OH, MY...

...IT'S GOTTEN VERY LATE.

TMP

...

GRROWL

HUH?

GRROWL

COME ON, GET UP.

WHAT'S YOUR STOMACH GROWLING FOR?!

GRROWL

18

16

WOBBLE...

GRR-ROWL

HFF HFF

GRROWL

HEH

I MEAN, HE NEVER BACKS DOWN.

HE ALWAYS WINS.

TMP

TMP

HEH

VIU, REALLY *IS* STRONG, AFTER ALL.

YOUR FATHER WAS A SHERIFF, WASN'T HE?

HUH?

SAY, ARE YOU GOING TO BE A SHERIFF AFTER ALL, VIU?

NO, I WON'T.

HFF HFF

GRRROWL

13

HE'S QUITE THE CHIP OFF THE OLD BLOCK.

WHEN HE GRADUATES, I'D LIKE TO MAKE HIM MY DEPUTY...TURN HIM INTO A FINE SHERIFF SOMEDAY.

I HEAR VIU WON IN THE TEEN DIVISION.

I'D BE WORRIED ABOUT HIM HAVING SUCH A DANGEROUS JOB, THOUGH.

I APPRECIATE YOUR OFFER, SHERIFF.

VIU'S A BOY, SO IT'S ONLY NATURAL FOR HIM TO BE ATTRACTED TO GUNS AND HOLSTERS.

BUT HE AND I ARE THE ONLY FAMILY WE HAVE, SO...

DID SOMETHING...

...HAPPEN?

CAN'T LET MY GUARD DOWN THESE DAYS. GOT TO STAY VIGILANT.

OOPS, I FORGOT. I WAS IN THE MIDDLE OF MY ROUNDS.

SHER-IFF.

HA HA. WELL, DON'T GET YOURSELF TOO WORKED UP.

JUST GIVE IT SOME THOUGHT, OKAY?

OKAY.

TMP TMP

BOOT and

12

SEE THAT?

FIRST PRIZE IS A GUN BELT.

THAT'S WHAT VIU IS AFTER.

FIRST PRIZE

READY.

YEAH!

G.R.I.P!

YEE HAW!

WELL, THE WINNER SEEMS OBVIOUS, BUT YOU NEVER KNOW!

YAY!

GRRR...

IT'LL BE OVER IN A SECOND.

PIECE OF CAKE.

YOU HAVE NO IDEA OF MY STRENGTH, DO YOU?!

YOU!

HE'S TAKING ON THE TEEN DIVISION WITH TOTAL DISREGARD FOR THE TEN-AND-UNDER DIVISION.

OH, MY!

OH, MY!

THERE WERE SHAKY MOMENTS, BUT HE MADE THE FINALS!

YEAH!

STOP INTRODUCING ME LIKE THAT.

HIS OLDER SISTER IS THAT HOT PRIMARY SCHOOLTEACHER, CISSY BANNES, AGE 21, AND SHE'S *SINGLE!*

YAAY!

YES! YES!

YEAH!

LISTEN VIU, DON'T GO THROUGH WITH THIS. IF YOU PUSH YOURSELF TOO HARD, YOU COULD GET HURT...

KILL THE GUY!

BREAK HIS ARM!

DO IT, VIU!

YOU, THERE! STOP EGGING HIM ON!

WHAT? DON'T YOU KNOW, MISS CISSY?

OH DEAR... I DON'T KNOW WHAT'S GOTTEN INTO HIM...

YAH!

CONTESTANTS, STEP FORWARD!

SHOOP

W-WAIT!

CHAPTER 1:
ENTER VIU BANNES

CHAPTER 1: ENTER VIU BANNES